THE
𝔊reen of the 𝔓eriod;

OR,

THE UNSUSPECTED FOE

IN THE

ENGLISHMAN'S HOME.

"Non ignara mali, miseris succurrere disco."
                                        VIRGIL.

LONDON:
ROUTLEDGE AND SONS,
BROADWAY, LUDGATE HILL.
—
1869.

This scarce antiquarian book is included in our special *Legacy Reprint Series*. In the interest of creating a more extensive selection of rare historical book reprints, we have chosen to reproduce this title even though it may possibly have occasional imperfections such as missing and blurred pages, missing text, poor pictures, markings, dark backgrounds and other reproduction issues beyond our control. Because this work is culturally important, we have made it available as a part of our commitment to protecting, preserving and promoting the world's literature. Thank you for your understanding.

THIS BOOK

IS DEDICATED, BY PERMISSION,

TO

THE RIGHT HON. WILLIAM F. COWPER, M.P.,

IN RECOGNITION OF

HIS PHILANTHROPIC EFFORTS TO SUPPRESS

THE EVIL WHICH THESE PAGES

ARE

DESIGNED TO EXPOSE.

PREFACE.

TRUTH is stranger than Fiction. Fiction is often nothing but the semblance, or the caricature of Truth. Facts are illustrations of Truth—the cropping up of great principles—seen, felt, welcome or unwelcome, accepted or opposed—but Facts still, stubborn Facts, to the end of the chapter.

Such Facts abound in these pages. Fiction there is none. Names of living persons, and of places, alone are disguised; such are never given, save when quoting from printed documents. Incidents of travel convey the reader, like our Railway Carriages, from one station to another. Narratives of startling incidents, such as thousands in our English Homesteads can verify, and will recognize as though they themselves were the *dramatis personæ*, are here recorded with historic faithfulness. Criticism is expected, invited, not shunned; not indeed the criticism of ignorance or prejudice, but the fair, honest criticism of an enlightened Public.

Contents.

CHAPTER I.
OUR STARTING-POINT.
Dover.
Our Tourists at Dover—The rejected Room—Mysterious Warnings—Why called the Green of the Period—Scheele's Green—Promised Information 1

CHAPTER II.
THE UNSUSPECTED FOE.
On Board the "Victoria."
Foreigners alive to this danger—Narrative of a Victim—Mrs. St. Alban at the Lakes—Decided preference for Green Paper—Roman Fever—A Strong Simile 7

CHAPTER III.
AN UNEXPECTED ALLY.
Crossing the Channel.
Dr. Hartington's Introduction—Sir Robert Chichester's Story—Symptoms of Arsenical Poisoning—Dr. Davis and Blind Erysipelas—Remedies suggested 13

CHAPTER IV.
THE VERDANT ASSASSIN.
Arrival at Calais.
The First Streak of Dawn—Fatal Symptoms—Approaching Paralysis—A *dernier Ressort*—Results Positive and Negative—Dr. Elliotson's Opinion—A graphic Description .. 20

CHAPTER V.
STORY OF A PHYSICIAN.
Detention at the Douane.

Paperhanger in Regent Street—Green Paper Analyzed—Testimony of a Paper Manufacturer—Three Tons of Arsenic per Week—Comparative Estimate of Mineral Poisons—Case of a Lady at Southampton 30

CHAPTER VI.
FOUR CHILDREN SACRIFICED.
The Rhine Falls.

Outline of a Swiss Tour—*Badinage* for Pay—Infanticide—Dr. Orton's Letter and Statement—Demand for Legislative Enactments—Liberty travestied 39

CHAPTER VII.
TAUGHT BY EXPERIENCE.
Lake of Constance.

Ridicule and Prejudices—Mrs. Conrad's Story—A Peripatetic Encyclopædia—Green Paper at Mont St. Bernard—Adventures at Northton-cum-Mire—Dr. Scotgur and the Verdant Assassin—Similarity of a Young Lady's Case .. 52

CHAPTER VIII.
NOBLE INVESTIGATORS.
Meyringen.

Artificial Florists and the Ladies' Sanitary Association—Cruel Poisonings—Professor Hoffmann's Letter to Mr. Cowper—Two Young Ladies at a Ball in Green Tarlatan Dresses—Fate of their Partners 63

CHAPTER IX.
THE LOGIC OF FACTS.
Under the Jungfrau.

Ennui at Interlachen—Story of Mrs. Mackenzie—Fate of a Paperhanger—Other Warnings and other Victims—Sir R. Chichester's Uncle at Youlcliff.. 74

CONTENTS.

CHAPTER X.
FURTHER REVELATIONS.
Grindelwald.
Crossing the Wengern Alp—Reminiscences of Grindelwald—Neuralgia—American Dentists and Arsenic—Shocking Result of sucking an Artificial Grape—Death of Two Children from Green Paper 83

CHAPTER XI.
A MATHEMATICAL DEMONSTRATION.
Lausanne.
Mrs. Fortescue's Visit to Llangwellan Castle—What causes Throat Affections—Effects of a Lucifer Match—Imperishable Nature of Strychnine and of Musk—Scheele's Green—Chambers' Journal · 93

CHAPTER XII.
ANOTHER VICTIM.
On the Linden.
Rencontre with Mr. Herbert—Mischief in a London Parish from the use of Green Paper—Special Case of a Lady—Warned, Convinced, Cured—Case of Another—Warning Unheeded 103

CHAPTER XIII.
VERDICT AGAINST THE POISONER.
Lake of the Four Cantons.
Medical Prejudices, their Cause and Effect—Dr. Millrod's New Hall Paper—"Warranted free from Arsenic"—Dr. Lapford's Story—Case of Mr. Wakley—Mr. Fortescue's Verdict 112

CHAPTER XIV.
INSURMOUNTABLE PREJUDICES.
Vallées des Ormonts.
Admiral Courtland—Is Green *Flock* Paper the most objectionable?—Testimony to the Medical Profession—Lady Chichester and Lady E. Howard—Does the Danger diminish by Time?—Professor Hoffmann's Test 122

CONTENTS.

CHAPTER XV.
AN ELECTRIC CURE.
Glaciers des Diablerets.

Plan des Isles—Laws of Electricity—A Remedial Agent—The Human Frame the Seat of War—Electro-Chemical Baths—Dr. Caplin's Discoveries—A Challenge—Heresy in Medicine—Ancient Cure for Scarlet Fever 132

CHAPTER XVI.
AUTHORITATIVE TESTIMONY.
Chamounix.

Dr. Morton's Case—Insanity produced by Green Paper—Another Medico convinced—The London Review—Dr. Orton's Testimony—Risk generally encountered at Hotels—Opinion of the Press 144

CHAPTER XVII.
DEATH ON THE WALLS.
Mont Blanc.

Hotel in North Devon—Two Children sacrificed to Scheele's Green—Post-mortem Examination—Electricity—Affection of the Heart—Visit in Wiltshire—Northend—Death of a Valued Servant—Green Wreaths and Erysipelas .. 155

CHAPTER XVIII.
OUR PARTING.
Geneva.

Old Woman from the Strand—Paperhanger's Testimony—Lady in Dublin—Young Lady at Tunbridge Wells—Little Boy lost in Diphtheria—Lady Maude's Case—Visit to a County Hospital—Arsenic at Railway Stations and everywhere—No *Ignis fatuus*—Adieux 164

APPENDIX.

A. B. C.—Notes 179
D.—Ophthalmia a result of the use of Arsenical Paperhangings 180

THE GREEN OF THE PERIOD.

CHAPTER I.

OUR STARTING-POINT.

> "See them guarded
> And safely brought to Dover; where, inshipped,
> Commit them to the fortune of the sea."
> *King Henry VI.*

> "I'll straightway to the moral of my story."
> *Dover.*

"CHICHESTER, how came you to disturb the Hotel out of its propriety last night? Henry Douglass tells me you quarrelled with your bed room, and insisted upon being shown half over the house before you could be satisfied. Were you afraid of ghosts?"

"Nay, as to ghosts proper, I had scarcely need to trouble myself, Fortescue," returned Sir Robert Chichester, "for we were so late in arriving, that if ghosts at Dover conduct themselves on the classic model, they would soon have vanished at the first cock-crowing. We have it on Shakespeare's authority that,

> "'at his warning,
> Whether in sea, or fire, in earth, or air,
> The extravagant and erring spirit hies
> To his confine.'

No, it was 'death on the walls' that scared me, and I would sooner have betaken myself to the stables than have established my quarters even for one night, in the arsenical den to which they at first assigned me."

"'Arsenical den!' 'Death on the walls!' in that enlivening green paper!" exclaimed Lord Henry Douglass. "I thought I heard you attempt to enlighten the bewildered chambermaid upon some scientific point, Chichester, but I really never thought you were in earnest. At all events, I appropriated to myself your rejected room, and here I am *in propriâ personâ*, none the worse for my night's rest.

"Long may you rejoice in your present immunity," returned Sir Robert; "but that danger lurks in the green of the period, rendering it fatal to some and unadvisable for all, I will try to convince you, for your own sake, before our tour is over. And if you have patience to hear me out, you will admit that I am not conjuring up 'spirits from the vasty deep.'"

"The green of the period!" said Lord Henry; "what makes you give it that cognomen, Chichester?"

"Simply because it is a green peculiar to the present day," replied Sir Robert; "a green utterly unlike its harmless predecessor in past days, and, one would fain hope, equally unlike what its successor in the future shall be, if we can only succeed in arousing public attention to its real nature; a green which our perverted tastes consider brilliant and beautiful, but which we should all shun if the veil were lifted and its character exposed. Still, it is *the* green of the period, which, like some of its contemporaries, is more showy than safe."

"But what of these green morocco chairs on which we are sitting, and those green satin curtains? My dear fellow, I am getting quite nervous," said Mr. Fortescue; "this is a bad beginning."

"Don't excite your nerves too soon," returned his friend, laughing, "for the dye once fixed, the green cannot harm us. It is only where the colour can escape that any danger arises."

"But I don't quite understand wherein the supposed danger lies," said Lord Henry. "Are all greens now-a-days noxious, or is the alarm confined to paper-hangings alone?"

"The danger is simply this: that, in order to produce this said green of the period, which varies in shade from a bright and brilliant tint to one as pale and delicate as can be desired, the paper manufacturers have introduced the use of a poisonous preparation known in the trade as 'Scheele's green,' but which is only another name for arsenic."

"But why is it more dangerous," inquired Lord Henry, "in paper hangings than in satin hangings?"

"Because the colour which embodies the poison comes off in the one case, and not in the other," replied Sir Robert. "Pass your hand along almost any wall you like, and more or less of the colour will adhere to your fingers. This coloured dust is being perpetually given off in the room, and if it contains poison must be necessarily injurious."

"But surely some papers are glazed, like a china teacup," said Mr. Fortescue.

"Here and there you may see a paper so very highly glazed that no dust will rub off, and the colour is, as it were, enamelled, and therefore innocuous; but this, as you will find on examination, is rare indeed. In nine hundred and ninety-nine cases out of every thousand it is otherwise; and the arsenical dust given off by the green papers of the present day is slaying its unsuspecting thousands."

"Well, perhaps it would be scarcely correct to say one has never before heard a word breathed against green paper," said Mr. Fortescue; "but certainly, until now, I have practically looked upon it in the light of a joke; and evidently both Henry Douglass and myself are awfully in the dark on the subject, Chichester, so you must set to work to enlighten us."

"You are really very good not to laugh at an idea so novel to you," replied his friend. "I can give you, if you wish it, plenty of illustrative proofs of the mischief against which I would warn you. But now breakfast is ready, and we must not spoil our host's equanimity by quarrelling with his food as well as with his green paper."

"*Eh bien!* reserve it for the crossing," said Mr. Fortescue; "we may all look greenish enough before we see the other side, if the threatening clouds of last night disturbed the waves as much as you must have disturbed the hotel."

The three friends had started for a six weeks' tour on the Continent, and were each sufficiently versed in the art of travel to know that half the enjoyment of the same consisted in a readiness to study the tastes, and even the *foibles* of their travelling companions. The idea of real danger from such a quarter was, if not ludicrous, yet somewhat questionable, to both Lord Henry and Mr. Fortescue, but each were willing to hear all the information their friend could give them, and before long the subject was resumed at their own request.

CHAPTER II.

THE UNSUSPECTED FOE.

"For lulled into a dangerous dream,
 We close infold a *foe*,
Who strikes when most secure we seem
 The *unsuspected* blow."
Cowper.

On Board the "Victoria."

"NEPTUNE is propitious, and we are ready," said Lord Henry a few hours later; "and when you have done pacing the *Victoria's* deck, Chichester, you have a fair opportunity of making converts of us."

"Or perverts," said Mr. Fortescue; "for it rather upsets one's preconceived notions of *otium cum dignitate* in travelling, to learn that henceforth one must ransack a whole hotel amidst a crowd of *garçons* and *filles de chambre*, headed by the astounded landlord or landlady, before one can repose in peace."

"It is better to run the gauntlet even to that extent, if needful, Fortescue," rejoined Sir Robert, "rather than awake with a sick headache, sore throat, smarting eyes, and all the attendant horrors induced by arsenical poisoning, when once it has really begun to take effect. However, to calm your fears at the present moment, I assure you that our opposite neighbours are far more alive than ourselves to the danger in question. In several of the States on the continent the manufacture of this poisonous paper is prohibited by law. Dr. C——, a leading physician in Paris, whom I consulted on my own case, assured me that, had my illness been incurred there instead of in London, I might have sued the maker of the paper, and have recovered damages to the extent of some thousands as compensation for the injury sustained."

"You actually have been a martyr, then, Chichester?" inquired Mr. Fortescue.

"I cannot claim the merits of martyrdom," replied Sir Robert, "for never was a less willing martyr; but victimized I certainly have been, having been brought as nearly to the grave, by means of your enlivening green paper, as could well be the case with any one who survives to tell the tale."

"A narrative of personal experience, then!" remarked Mr. Fortescue, "so let us have it forthwith. Apology and preface may alike be dispensed with."

"You are really prepared for the infliction?" asked his friend. "Remember, it will contain a catalogue of half the ills that flesh is heir to."

"Agreed," said both the friends.

"And if we are converted to your views," added Lord Henry, "shall we stand first on your list, or have you succeeded in convincing many others?"

"Well, I usually find experience to be the best teacher," replied Sir Robert. "Fortescue, do you remember my wife's mother?"

"Indeed I do; once to have had the pleasure of Mrs. St. Alban's acquaintance is never to forget her. I trust she has not suffered from this alarming paper?"

"But very slightly," answered Sir Robert, "and only on one occasion, yet that one was sufficient to remove all her previous incredulity. She was making a tour at the Lakes two or three years since in company with her sons, and, on reaching a small hotel, she was taken so ill in the night that they were unable to continue their route. Next day her maid, after sitting some time in the room, complained likewise of queer sensations, when it flashed across them that the bright green paper with which the room was hung might be the delinquent. My mother-in-law asked to have a piece of the paper, and sent it for analyzation, when the arsenic was only too apparent. The argument of these forty-eight hours proved more potent than my words."

"Well, congratulate Mrs. St. Alban from me," said Mr. Fortescue, "on having made the discovery, without paying a penalty so dear as that which you speak of, and which we are now all anxiety to hear."

"First tell us," said Lord Henry, "did you knowingly run your head into the danger?"

"By no means," replied Sir Robert. "I thought —if, indeed, I troubled myself to reason on the subject at all—that Nature, having decided on the colour of green as being most suitable for the eyes out of doors, it must be equally so indoors, and took special pains to have a green flock paper for my library in every house I took. Strange symptoms, even then, manifested themselves, and on one occasion resulted in a fever, which my medical man, for want of a better name, called 'Roman fever;' but I now believe 'green paper fever' would have been its more appropriate designation."

"Did you at that time discover arsenic to be the cause of your illness?" inquired Mr. Fortescue.

"No, nor for years after," replied Sir Robert. "Soon after my recovery I took a new house, in which my bedroom and dressing-room were already hung with this brilliant apple-green paper. For the library, my choice again fell on the green flock paper; and here my arsenical story properly begins. The sufferings consequent upon this state of things, which were now coiling me, as it were, in their grasp, day and night, were as perplexing in their symptoms, as they were indescribable in their nature, and baffled the skill of the first physicians in London, many of whom I consulted in vain."

"Your case must have been very peculiar," said Lord Henry. "All cannot be equally affected by the said poison."

"All are not alike susceptible to malaria of any nature," replied Sir Robert. "Take a man ill with small-pox, cholera, or scarlet fever, and place him in the midst of a large assembly: it is morally certain that a very considerable number of those present will not be injuriously affected by his unwelcome intrusion; yet it is equally certain that his advent will be attended with danger to some, and with risk to all, even though they remain in the room with him but half an hour."

"That is a very strong simile, Chichester," said Mr. Fortescue, "and leads one to question what infection is. I suppose, in such a case, it is a poisoned atmosphere, which some constitutions are, and others are not, physically capable of resisting. But how does this bear upon your own case?"

"Simply because my own wellnigh fatal illness was caused by inhaling a poisoned atmosphere, that of arsenic, which I think you will see as my story proceeds."

CHAPTER III.

AN UNEXPECTED ALLY.

"Experience teacheth many things, and all men are his
    scholars;
Yet is he a strange tutor, unteaching that which he hath
    taught."
Proverbial Philosophy.

Crossing the Channel.

"PARDON me, gentlemen, if I intrude upon your conversation," said a voice near the last speaker.

Our travellers turned, and saw a gentleman of prepossessing exterior, who had been leaning over the side of the steamer near them, apparently absorbed in the contemplation of the waves.

" Pardon my interruption," he continued; "but I have accidentally overheard the subject of your conversation, and I should much like to hear your promised story."

" Pray do so," said the three friends.

" Your request," added Sir Robert, "involves the

supposition that you are familiar with the dangers of green paper. Is it so?"

"Only quite recently, which makes me the more anxious to hear any facts bearing upon the subject. I am a medical man of some practice in London; and one case, in particular, which has just come under my own notice, has made me feel it necessary to be alive to this newly-discovered danger."

"Indeed! Perhaps you will rather favour us with the case in point?" said Sir Robert.

"Willingly, when my turn arrives," replied the new comer; "but you must not let me disturb your story, or I shall consider myself an intruder."

"Without further circumlocution, then, Chichester, to your narrative," said Mr. Fortescue; "or we shall be in the grasp of the *douanières* before you begin."

"Well, I will be as brief as possible. Perhaps no ordinary warnings would have sufficed to convince me; but each morning, on awakening, as soon as I had established myself in my verdant quarters, I felt the strangest sensations. Smarting of the eyes and soreness of the throat and mouth were amongst the earliest symptoms. Sometimes these vanished, or were forgotten by the time breakfast was over; for, happily, our dining-room had an oak paper, untinctured with arsenic. But when I retreated to the library, with its green flock paper, my troubles recommenced. Oppression over the eyes, inducing heaviness or headache, constantly rendered reading or writing out of the question; lassitude in every form, languor and debility, which all the energy I could command failed at times to control, threatened to make life intolerable. The cause and effect alike continued for about three years, without so much as being suspected."

"I must confess you have reason to speak strongly against this subtle foe," said Lord Henry; "but did you obtain no relief during all that period?"

"Only, from time to time, in flight. Had my sufferings being incessant," continued Sir Robert, "I really think that death, which I fully expected, would have terminated them; and the only light which the *post-mortem* examination would have thrown upon my demise would have been, 'Death induced by poison, but by whom administered there is no evidence to show.'"

"You spoke of taking eminent advice," said Dr. Hartington, their new friend. "Did no one suggest the possible origin of your illness?"

"Not one," replied Sir Robert. "I tried in succession allopathic, homœopathic, and hydropathic practitioners; but not one even suspected the nature of the irritant. I am bound to say that I consulted most of them at their own residences, not at my own; consequently very few of them ever saw the said paper. Dr. B——, of Mayfair, repeatedly questioned me as to the state of the drainage of my house and neighbourhood, asking if any manufactory, or any miasma, or anything prejudicial to health, existed in the vicinity. He said I was evidently under the influence of some poison, but his surmises never pointed to the actual cause."

"Have you described to us all your symptoms?" asked Dr. Hartington.

"No, indeed," said Sir Robert. "They would weary you as much as they perplexed myself and my medical advisers. Suffice it to say that I was never free from English cholera when at home; that I was a martyr to indigestion; that I suffered awfully from neuralgia; that I had strange and unaccountable swellings, local and general; that I had threatenings of dropsy; that my heart was supposed to be affected; and, finally, that a paralytic stroke was considered inevitable!"

"My dear Chichester, you almost take away one's breath," said Mr. Fortescue. "I do remember hearing of your having been very ill, but just about that time we did not chance to cross each other's orbit, and to look at you now one would imagine illness and you had been life-long strangers. How on earth were you resuscitated from such a pitiable state of things?"

"Certainly it was pitiable enough, Fortescue, and life was a burden. One symptom in addition I must mention, for on that occasion my medical attendant had the opportunity of seeing the green paper and discovering the cause, which he failed to do. I was seized one night with strange giddiness and faintings, and sent early the next morning for Dr. Davis, feeling too ill to rise. My face on this occasion was so swelled and disfigured, that scarcely a feature could be recognized. Dr. Davis came, and was evidently posed by the contradictory nature of my malady. He said it was not erysipelas proper, but christened it 'blind erysipelas' for the nonce, and made minute investigations as to whether I had poisoned myself by smoking bad cigars, or by any other proceedings equally wide of the mark. I was all the time lying in bed actually environed by this 'green of the period,' which was sapping my life, and he never suspected it. He gave me strong doses of quinine, and advised me as usual to go away for change of air, which as usual set me up *pro tem.*"

"I am afraid, sir," said Lord Henry, addressing Dr. Hartington, "you will indict us as libelling, or conniving at libel, against your professional brethren."

"As yet they have had fair play," said Dr. Hartington, smiling; "and I can at least answer for myself that I am open to conviction, and that I feel deeply interested in your friend's remarkable account. By 'blind erysipelas' I believe your medical man meant poisoned blood, and as to the effect, and the medicine he employed on the occasion, he was doubtless right. Was this the climax?"

"No, far from it," said Sir Robert, "though I have since been assured that this was a crisis which at the time saved my life. I continued for another twelvemonth alternating between attacks equally unaccountable, including boils, tumours, &c., &c., and partial recoveries induced by change of air. These recoveries, however, never long survived a return to my own house. The servants used to tell my wife that they dreaded to see me come home, for I had never been seated in my library a single hour before some one of the multifarious symptoms reappeared. It was settled beyond a question that the library was somehow in fault. The boards were more than once taken up; the drains were again and again examined, and a clean bill of health returned; but the real enemy—the green of the period—was never once called to the bar."

"Were you the only sufferer?" asked Lord Henry; "for surely, if every one were similarly affected, the manufacture of green paper would have been long since abandoned."

"Comparatively few are, I believe, quite as susceptible to malaria and poisonous influences as I am," said Sir Robert; "and Lady Chichester was quite unconscious at the time of deriving any injury. That is, however, no argument in its favour, for I believe it is a known fact that of all poisons none is so uncertain and so variable in its operations as arsenic."

"True," said Dr. Hartington; "and even in one and the same individual, according to his physical state, it produces very different results. Usually the nerves of the face, head, and throat become first affected. I am quite curious to hear the diagnosis of your case *in extenso*."

CHAPTER IV.

THE VERDANT ASSASSIN.

"Be aware of the smiling enemy that openly sheatheth his weapon,
But mingleth poison in secret with the sacred salt of hospitality."
Proverbial Philosophy.

"Away with him to prison—where is the provost?"
Measure for Measure.

Arrival at Calais.

"THE darkest hour precedes the dawn," replied Sir Robert Chichester; "so a dawn was mercifully at hand in my case; but fearful was the struggle before the light broke in on my sufferings. About a year after my 'blind erysipelas' had so enigmatically transformed me, I was again very ill, and this time we decided on visiting the continent in hopes of obtaining alleviation. Hardly had we reached Paris when the clouds which had been so long gathering, to speak metaphorically, burst. I was unable to rouse myself to take an interest in anything, and the use of my limbs was so rapidly failing, that my only desire was to return to England."

"You attribute this melancholy state of things actually to the green paper?" asked Mr. Fortescue.

"To the arsenic which had been so long absorbed into the system, I do undoubtedly," answered his friend; "and since the discovery of the cause, all the medical men whom I had previously consulted have also agreed in so doing."

"How was relief obtained?" asked Dr. Hartington, "for science has as yet failed to discover any chemical antidote to arsenic."

"Accidentally, or rather, I should say providentially," replied Sir Robert, "for it became a neck-and-neck race between life and death. I returned to England *viâ* Brighton, and there, by a strange fatality, took up my quarters where my bedroom was papered with the most virulent yet the most brilliant of greens. Swelling of the whole frame then came on, as though I had been bitten by a serpent. Still my return had been apparently accompanied by beneficial effects, and for a while I was enabled to walk about, though with difficulty. Gradually, but perceptibly, all the vital powers declined. In addition to the best and most skilful medical treatment, I had placed myself in the hands of a medical rubber, and if any dependence can be placed upon one's feelings in such a case, I should say that to his rubbing, humanly speaking, I owe the arrest of a fatal termination when life was ebbing.

"In this state I continued for three months," continued Sir Robert, "each week the end being evidently nearer, till at length I was unable to walk across my room alone. One night I took a last farewell of my wife, believing I should not live till morning. She held a private consultation with the doctors, and has since told me that all the comfort they could bestow was to say that a stroke of paralysis was imminent, and could by no means be averted; that their hope was that it might only affect some limb, and they kindly tried to soothe her fears by saying, when it had assumed that definite form, they could better tell how to deal with it."[1]

"How awful!" exclaimed Lord Henry.

"I survived the night, however," continued Sir Robert, "and the next day a bright thought struck me, to the effect that the Water-system, as all else had failed, might as well be tried."

"I was not aware that hydropathy had erected

one of its fanes at Brighton," remarked Dr. Hartington.

"There was one of very modest pretensions at that time in a private house," said Sir Robert, "and I accordingly determined to send for the doctor, and see what he could do for me. It was a desperate venture; for on mentioning my intention to my medical adviser, he solemnly warned my wife that if I persisted in trying the Water-system in any form, I was a dead man."

"And you persisted nevertheless!" exclaimed Mr. Fortescue.

"I was too ill to have their opinion communicated to me," replied Sir Robert; "but, had I known it, I should still have felt that, as a dying man, I was at liberty to try anything that offered a reasonable hope of alleviation."

"And you owed your cure to your new doctor?" inquired Mr. Fortescue.

"I did not say that," answered his friend; "but this was the first link in the chain which drew me out of the slough of despond. The doctor ordered me baths at some unconscionable hour in the morning, which required the attendance of a bathman; this necessitated my sleeping in another room, which was happily free from any taint of green paper, and my cure was negatively begun."

"And what was the positive result?" asked Lord Henry.

"That a change for the better was visible from that very day," replied Sir Robert. "The various hydropathic remedies prescribed tended to draw the poison by degrees out of the system. I no longer imbibed the arsenic either by day or night; and in a month I was sufficiently restored to venture on a journey to Malvern, there to continue the cure under more scientific auspices."

"I cannot say how much your case interests me," said Dr. Hartington. "I little expected, at the outset of my travels, to gather so important an addition to my medical lore. May I ask what length of time was required to eradicate the poison which you had, as you say, imbibed?"

"That question is not easy to answer," said Sir Robert, "as you will gather from my subsequent story. I continued under the treatment at Malvern for about three months, and then, by the advice of my doctor, I travelled for some weeks before returning home."

"I do not yet understand," said Mr. Fortescue,

when or how you ascertained beyond a doubt that arsenic was the delinquent. You denounce it *vi et armis*, but how do you establish a *casus belli* ?"

"We are coming to that point," said Sir Robert. "Upon returning home, I reoccupied the same rooms as before, with the beautiful papers which had so nearly cost me my life. Again a metallic taste and smarting of the eyes assailed me on awakening, and prostration of strength alarmed me throughout the day. Attributing all to my recent illness, I merely concluded I was not so far restored as I had hoped. We therefore contemplated going abroad for several months, but previously went to consult Dr. Elliotson, of known skill and deserved celebrity. He heard my story, was evidently puzzled at my case, said I ought to be well, and could not see that I should gain anything from travel; prescribed a tonic, and hoped soon to see me again."

"Still no allusion to arsenic?" inquired Lord Henry.

"Never a hint," replied Sir Robert. "I went home, determined to fancy myself cured, and to exercise unbounded faith in this tonic. But, alas! each morning I but woke to a consciousness that

I was *not* cured, and that my old symptoms were slowly but surely returning. One day a sudden thought flashed across my mind, that rumours of danger arising from green paper had certainly been afloat, though somehow I had never connected it, however distantly, with my own illness. The idea was too new and startling to digest at a moment's notice, but too important not to be investigated when once it had arisen. I shifted my quarters the following night to a room innocent of green paper, or green in any part of the paper, and awoke next morning without any of the unpleasant sensations I have described. By degrees we remembered that the dressing-room and study were similarly decorated, and that if one room was in fault all were in the same class. For four days I carefully abstained from re-entering any of them, and by the end of that time I felt so well that I entirely forgot my supposed discovery, and attributed the change to the new tonic."

"Your description is really capital," exclaimed Mr. Fortescue, "but it fluctuates between a comedy and a tragedy. I must confess there was evidently no preconceived ideas on your part which would establish the fact whether it existed or not. I suppose, in this state of blissful ignorance, you soon again plunged into danger?"

"Yes," replied Sir Robert, "*in medias res*. I again took possession of my library, and in less than one hour nausea came on, accompanied by swelling of the lip, and livid spots upon it, which I had frequently remarked before."

"Is it possible?" exclaimed Mr. Fortescue and Lord Henry at once.

"Only too true," said Sir Robert; "and upon the strength of my discovery I went off to Dr. Elliotson, to see if the evidence were conclusive to his mind. He listened to my story, and then requested that I would recapitulate all the symptoms I could recall, which had been so mysterious during the last few years. I did so, and as each symptom or incident came in review before him, he capped it with the invariable conclusion, 'Arsenic,' 'Arsenic again,' 'that was arsenic,' 'clearly arsenic,' &c., &c."

"Elliotson was really convinced?" asked Dr. Hartington.

"His remark was," replied Sir R. Chichester, "'Never in all my life have I met with so striking a case. The English cholera, and the mysterious so-called erysipelas, undoubtedly saved your life at the time. Few would have been so affected as you have been, and survived to tell the story.' He was of opinion that Turkish baths, which I had been taking of late, had acted most beneficially, but warned me that I must expect to feel the effects for some time to come."

"You really should have made your case public to warn others," said Lord Henry.

"Well, Elliotson did beg I would write out my case fully and let him have it, when he would have endorsed it and sent it to the *Times;* but partly from having a great deal on my hands at that moment, which left me but little time to comply with his request, and partly from seeing the strange prejudice and unwillingness to believe which exists on the subject, I never did so."

"Did you state your case to your other medical advisers?" asked Dr. Hartington.

"I did so to each one, and every one allowed, with more or less grace, that the cause which they had failed to discover was undoubtedly arsenical poisoning. 'Why did you not find that out before?' I asked Dr. B——. 'Simply because our attention had not then been called to the mischief in that particular form,' was his reply."

"You are certainly proving your words to a demonstration that danger lurks in green paper," said Lord Henry, "yet somehow it seemed at first sight as if it were a sort of danger at which one should blink."

"It is well enough to acquiesce in the inevitable," replied Sir Robert; "but surely unnecessary that we should ourselves prepare the poisoned chalice, or hold it to our lips."

"Well, they say truth is stranger than fiction,' remarked Mr. Fortescue. "After what you have gone through, Chichester, the marvel is to find you still amongst the living. No wonder even the ghost of green paper alarms you, as a burnt child dreads the fire. I shall go home and examine all my paper hangings, and if there is the smallest doubt respecting them, I will have at least one room specially papered for your reception."

"Thanks, my dear fellow; but here we are almost at the pier. They are hauling up all the passengers' luggage, and we must look sharp, or no one knows what may become of *nos baggages*."

"Nevertheless, we must not forget," said Lord Henry, turning to Dr. Hartington, "to call upon you for your promised story, as soon as we are upon *terra firma*."

CHAPTER V.

STORY OF A PHYSICIAN.

"Discern the fraud beneath the specious lure,
Prevent the danger, or prescribe the cure."—*Cowper*.

Detention at the Douane.

"My story is a very brief one," said Dr. Hartington, when the travellers again met in the outer room of the *Douane*, "and as one knows from past experience that we may be kept here some time awaiting the pleasure of these Messieurs, I will, if you please, give it you now."

"We are all attention," said the friends.

"I am thankful for your unexpected aid," added Sir Robert Chichester, "in awakening the minds of these gentlemen to a hitherto unappreciated danger."

"Some few months since," said the Doctor, "I was suddenly summoned to the house of a paper-hanger in Regent Street, whose servant, I was told, had been taken very ill, and they feared she was poisoned.

"I lost no time in attending her, and the first thing which caught my eye was the brilliant green paper with which the room was hung. I pointed it out to the persons around her, saying that although no case had (as far as I was aware) ever occurred in my own practice, yet they must have heard what was said as to the injurious effect of Scheele's green. I therefore advised her immediate removal into another room, where I prescribed for her, and had the satisfaction of soon subduing the symptoms which had so alarmed her employers."

"Were they really those of a person who had been poisoned by arsenic?" asked Sir Robert Chichester.

"Yes; she had complained of severe pain and a coldness, occasionally of palpitations of the heart and syncope, and now the vomiting which had come on was very violent."

"Did you analyze the paper?" inquired Lord Henry.

"I requested to have some of it for the purpose of analyzation," replied Dr. Hartington, "and sent it to Dr. T——, the well-known analytical chemist. I still have by me the results obtained, and which struck me forcibly. He first showed the proportion of arsenious acid (commonly known as arsenic) contained in the paper; secondly, how much arsenic would be given off every hour; and lastly, he made a calculation of the amount of impalpable poisonous dust which would mingle with every cubic foot of the atmosphere in the room. Since that time I have, as you may believe, been very fully alive to the possible danger arising from green paper."

"But how do you account for the fact," said Lord Henry, "that I encountered this danger last night, and still survive to tell the tale?"

"Its most inveterate opponents only view it as a *slow* poison," returned the physician, smiling; "and it would be an awful thing could it have made quite so rapid a termination of your lordship's earthly career."

"Is not arsenic used by some medicos as a medicine?" inquired Mr. Fortescue.

"Not only by some, but by all; and an invaluable medicine it is in certain cases. I should be sorry indeed if its abuse were ever used as an effectual argument against its use. But you can easily imagine that if you take the most valuable medicine in the pharmacopœia, and use it daily as an article of food, inhaling it constantly, its value would cease. Especially if you apply this argument to a known poison, let it be taken in portions ever so infinitesimal, the effects must be, in the long run, excessively injurious."

"Then you do not advise the adoption in any case of these favourite papers?" said Lord Henry.

"I would eschew the fatal green if only from motives of humanity," replied the doctor, "for though nineteen out of twenty may perhaps use it with comparative impunity, the twentieth may lose the enjoyment of life, if not life itself, from the indulgence of a mere whim."

"I only wish all your professional brethren held equally enlightened sentiments," remarked Sir Robert Chichester, "but I must confess the amount of ignorance and prejudice I have encountered amongst medical men when trying to warn my friends, who were evidently suffering from this very cause, has been prodigious. Even Dr. Campbell, whom I consulted in my own case, and who was subsequently obliged to own that I had been under the influence of arsenic, thinks so lightly of it that he has it in his own house. In the dining-room there is a pretty subdued green, and one at least of his rooms upstairs is papered with the undeniable green of the period. His wife, a most charming woman, is always ailing, and suffers from utter prostration of strength, yet he laughs to scorn any hint that the removal of the green paper might, if only as an experiment, be advisable."

"We certainly are not infallible," said Dr. Hartington; "but I must say, in extenuation of my brethren, that they but share the public apathy and incredulity on the subject, until, as in my own case, something occurs to startle their slumbers. I was lately speaking to my landlord about it, and advising him not to allow green papers to be put up in his houses. He told me that a friend of his was a large paper-manufacturer in the north, and that on a recent visit to him he had questioned him as to the rumours which were in circulation respecting the use of arsenic. My landlord had previously been incredulous as to its being employed to any extent, but the ready reply of his friend was, 'I can only tell you that *I* use about three tons of arsenic a week.'"

"Is it possible!" exclaimed the whole party.

"Such, he assured me, was the information he received," replied the doctor; "and mark the manufacturer's excuse. When asked by his friend how he could be guilty of such a wholesale poisoning system, his answer was, 'If the public are such fools as to require it, we must make it. If I did not supply the demand, other paper-makers would.'"

"Do you suppose arsenic is used in every paper containing green?" asked Mr. Fortescue.

"My landlord said he put this very question to the manufacturer, who replied that there was no green in any of his papers that was not produced by the employment of arsenic."

"I am afraid you are but too just in your implied strictures on an unthinking public. But ought not the medical faculty, like philosophers of old, to endeavour to guide public opinion in such a matter?" inquired Lord Henry Douglass.

Some of us do venture to swim against the current, but others perhaps do not like to commit themselves to an opinion evidently distasteful to the public, and shield their consciences behind the known fact that many are comparatively unaffected by mineral poisons. Of arsenic, for instance, which one person may swallow as much as ten grains and survive the dose, another would scarcely take half a grain with similar impunity.

"A strong argument against playing with edged

tools, certainly," remarked Mr. Fortescue, "as we seem to be doing in the matter of this green paper."

"Indeed it is so," said Dr. Hartington, "we are actually trifling with a poison. As regards the pernicious influence of arsenic as at present under discussion, it is impossible for any one on earth to say without a trial, how much or how little will produce a given effect, neither how it will affect the inmates of a house, nor whether it will affect them in any degree. But let me impress this upon you, that where it finds a subject susceptible to its influence, arsenic acts almost instantaneously, and therefore by such an one it cannot be too rigorously avoided."

"Have any further instances come under your own observation?" asked Sir Robert Chichester.

"Yes," answered Dr. Hartington, "since I have become alive to the danger, I have detected its workings in cases where I might previously not have suspected it. A lady consulted me a few weeks since, whose history was most melancholy. Her husband had taken a house at Southampton, where the sitting-room was papered with a light green paper. Shortly after removing thither, both were attacked with sore throats, but the husband, who was out all day, suffered comparatively little. The poor lady lost her strength, appetite, and powers of digestion, and languished for months under what was supposed to be an internal complaint. She came up to London and consulted me. I found her mucous membrane in so inflamed and diseased a state throughout, that the coats of the stomach were destroyed, and I have but little hopes of her ever being restored to health. At my request she sent for some of the paper, and I analyzed it, with the usual results."

"You have no doubt that this accounted for her sufferings?" asked Mr. Fortescue.

"I have no doubt of this poison having become imbibed into the system, and originating her illness," replied the doctor.

"I am sorry our routes diverge so shortly," said Mr. Fortescue, "and that we shall lose the benefit of your conversation, but as regards our acquisition of knowledge in this particular department, my friend here is so thoroughly up in it that I expect we shall be indoctrinated into all the mysteries of green paper before our return to England."

"Don't expect me to obtrude my opinions upon you," said Sir Robert; "you would vote me a bore;

and gladly as I would see the green of the period placed in the Index Expurgatorius, I do not mean to inflict any more of my sufferings and researches upon my fellow-travellers."

"But we really wish to be informed and enlightened," said Lord Henry, "and on reasonable occasions you must indulge us with your discoveries."

"I mean to take notes *pro bono publico*," said Mr. Fortescue; when suddenly the door was thrown open, and further discussion was cut short.

CHAPTER VI.

FOUR CHILDREN SACRIFICED.

"Dead! dead! Is there no one to weep?
Dead! dead! How it makes one's blood creep
To think of those murdered *infants.*"
Blighted Pasque-flowers.

The Rhine Falls.

"How now, Douglass? do you regret entering Switzerland under the roar of these magnificent Rhine Falls?" asked Mr. Fortescue, who had been watching with delight his friend's enthusiastic admiration of them. "Bottle up a little of your ecstasy, old fellow, for you will see finer falls than these in the land of the mountain and the flood."

"Regret is inadmissible at this moment," answered Lord Henry; "and though I had proposed our crossing over the Jura, which we can still do in returning, I believe with you, Fortescue, that this is after all the best entrance into Switzerland. At least, if one had just come from the grandest features which this land of surpassing beauty has to offer, one might perhaps think the Falls of the Rhine, and the Lake of Constance comparatively tame."

"Which view of the subject is undoubtedly out of the question after coming from Paris, with all its wear and tear of sight-seeing, and friend-seeing," rejoined Sir Robert Chichester. "The stillness and quiet of this spot is delicious, and I am in no hurry to leave it."

"Had we not better plan out our route?" said Mr. Fortescue, "I think we agreed you were to be cicerone, were you not, Chichester?"

"I don't think I gave any promise to that effect," returned Sir Robert; "but suppose while we rest here, we con it over, map in hand. I like avoiding beaten tracks as much as possible, if any route in Switzerland can be said to be otherwise. *Sommes-nous d'accord?*"

"Decidedly," said both his companions.

"What say you, then, to a rough outline, somewhat to this effect, to be varied of course according to circumstances? From the Lake of Constance *viâ* Glarus, Altorf, and Meyringen, to Interlachen.

Thence, after seeing the two lakes which it bridges across, to Lauterbrunnen and Grindelwald. Over the Furka Pass to Hospenthal on Mount St. Gotthard. Descend over the Devil's Bridge to Fluelen, for Lucerne. Thence to Thun, and, steaming down its pretty lake, to Chateau D'Œx for excursions into the Simmenthal and the valleys of Les Ormonts, including a peep at the Diablerets. Descend on Martigny for a visit to Chamounix and Mont Blanc, crossing the Tête Noir, and returning *viâ* Cormayeur, making a *détour* to pay our respects to the monks of St. Bernard. We can wind up with Geneva and Lausanne.

"Or, if you incline to a peep into Italy, and are as fond as I am of mountain passes, cross the Simplon to Lago Maggiore. Then, visiting Lago Lugano, and the fairy Lake of Como, cross the Splugen, and the Via Mala, to Coire, Pfäffers, and Ragatz. Home by the Lake of Zurich, and, if you please, Neuchâtel and the Jura. Now, what do you think of your route?"

"Excellent, splendid, charming, feasible!" exclaimed Lord Henry. "It's capital having a fellow at hand to save one the trouble of deciding one's own route. Are you agreed, Fortescue?"

"Indeed, I think we could hardly do better, if only our time would permit us to carry it out," replied Mr. Fortescue; "there are, in addition, various excursions of interest which we can visit *en route*. By the way, Chichester, I don't know that it exactly bears upon the point, but surely there was a subject almost as extensive as our travels, upon which you promised to enlighten us; and since we left Calais, I declare I have never heard another word about your arsenical discoveries."

"I never now causelessly intrude 'the green of the period' upon my friends," answered Sir Robert; "I have suffered so much from it that it almost seems egotistical to allude to it. Moreover, so few realize or believe in the danger, that one has to stand fire, and endless *badinage* is my usual pay."

"But, indeed, we were both startled by your facts, were we not, Douglass?" said his friend, "which is half way to being convinced. So, Chichester, now that we are once more at rest, do be good enough to resume the thread of your narrative."

"If you both really wish to hear more about it," said Sir Robert, "I have some extracts on the subject in my pocket-book which I have cut out of the newspapers from time to time, and which I would prefer reading to you to giving you my own personal experience."

"Why, has it actually engaged public attention to that extent?" asked Mr. Fortescue.

"Yes; from time to time, as I just said, when deaths occur from the use of green paper, inquests are held, and astounding statements are made, and for a few days public attention is aroused, and people are alarmed; but it is forgotten again, the green grows over their graves, and arsenic is soon as much in vogue as ever."

"*Par example!* Well, I think it is high time our apathy should be disturbed. So now, Chichester, for your extracts," said Lord Henry.

"One of the first extracts I have," resumed Sir Robert, "refers to the cases of four children, who all died within a period of two months with strong symptoms of arsenical poisoning, stated to have been caused by inhaling the emanations from green paper-hangings. The leading facts in the case were noticed in a paragraph and letter which appeared in the *Times*.

"Dr. Orton, of Stepney, who attended the deathbed of the fourth child, in giving his evidence on the inquest, said:—

'"He was called to deceased on the 3rd of April, and found her suffering from extreme prostration. He thought the symptoms exhibited by the child very strange, and questioned the mother about the other children. She said that they had all been attacked in the same way, and had ultimately died of soreness of the throat, which had been attributed to diphtheria. He prescribed tonics, but without much effect. He then noticed the green paper on the wall, and could see a marked connexion between the symptoms exhibited by the deceased and the other children, and those caused by arsenical poisoning. He made a *post mortem* examination, and found that the stomach presented streaks of inflammation, but was otherwise healthy. The intestines were also inflamed. The other organs were healthy. He found no traces of disease to account for death.'

"'Dr. Letheby, Professor of Chemistry at the London Hospital, said he had received from Dr. Orton the stomach and viscera of deceased, and also a certain portion of green paper. He found that the latter contained arsenic, loosely adherent, in the proportion of three grains to the square foot. There was no glaze, and the poison could be very easily rubbed off. He examined the stomach and viscera, but could not find arsenic. The symptoms described by Dr. Orton were those of arsenical poisoning. He had known effects of the same kind produced by the poisonous powder from such papers being absorbed and inhaled while floating in the atmosphere; though he could not trace arsenic in the system, yet he should say in the absence of disease that death might have been caused by arsenic.'

"In cross-examination, Dr. Letheby went on to say:—

"'Owing to the absorption of the poison being gradual, it was possible that the traces might be wanting, though the effect would be fatal. The fact that the children were not sleeping in the room did not make much difference. He had known two children in Hackney die from arsenical poisoning imbibed while playing for a few hours daily in their father's library. Arsenic would not produce diphtheria, but it would soreness of throat.'

"'Dr. Orton, recalled, said he had no hesitation in saying that deceased died from chronic poisoning, by arsenic taken into the system in minute quantities. Cases were on record in which arsenic known to have been taken, could not be traced after death.'

"Dr. Orton also addressed the following letter to the public prints, which I will read to you:—

"'Sir,—If any doubt should remain in the minds of your readers respecting the deadly influence of arsenical green paper-hangings since the recent investigation at Limehouse, will you allow me, as the surgeon who was called in professionally to attend one, and only one—the last of the four children—to state as briefly as possible a few facts relating thereto, and which have not hitherto been evolved in the evidence?

"'I pass over the simple statement of the mother —in itself all that was requisite to establish the case —in conjunction with the medical evidence, and I will overlook the conclusive testimony of so eminent a man as Dr. Letheby, confining my remarks only to a popular view of the question.

"'1. The mother declared that her children had always been healthy up to Christmas last; that "she had never had a doctor in the house, except on her own account, in her life," till the children had the measles, followed by diphtheria, in January, February, and March last.

"'2. That this green paper at Christmas was first placed on the walls, and then, and not till then, was the beginning of the sorrows. The father, mother, and all the children began to sicken. The symptoms, more or less, were smarting of the eyes, irritation of the nostrils, headache (over the brows in particular), soreness of the mouth and throat, with occasional sharp pains over the bowels. There was also a constant rubbing of the upper lip and nose, and picking of the mouth.

"'3. The antiseptic properties of arsenic are well known. It is used largely by naturalists in the preservation of birds. Now, mark the force of truth. Seven days had elapsed since the death, and yet the body of this child was undecomposed. The father was present, and noticed there was no effluvium and no discoloration whatever.

"'4. The undertaker also noticed specially that all the three preceding children, after being four days dead, were in a like condition; while all other bodies, under the same circumstances, emitted the most offensive odour.

"'5. Abdominal pain is a marked symptom. The third child had this severely. Ask the mother, and she will tell the inquirer that the fourth and last was seized just like the third, and "what killed one killed the other."

"'6. That arsenic was not found is nothing to the purpose. There are notorious cases on record, in which none of this mineral has been found on analysis, and yet the poisoning unquestioned.

"'7. The green paper has been removed from this house in Tomlin's Terrace now upwards of three weeks; and here again, Sir, I ask you to mark the result. That pain of the head, that smarting of the eyes, and occasional twinge, have now ceased! Those symptoms which father, mother, and all the children had, on introduction of the green paper, have now wholly disappeared!

"'In conclusion, Sir, permit me to say that the effects of this arsenical paper, though unsuspected, are not uncommon. I believe that much baffling disease, especially throat affections, frequently owe their origin to this cause. If your columns were open to the discussion, you would have a host of medical and other correspondents bearing testimony to the force of my observations. I have frequently been called to the sick-bed, and trace the evil to the paper, and nothing else. I have known a family of children sickening for a while; they have been sent into the country, and got well. They have been brought home again, and again taken ill. The paper has been removed, and sickness has ceased. A few days ago, in my own neighbourhood, a person, in cleaning her house gently brushed over the green paper on the walls. In an hour or two she and her husband were seized with pains in the eyes and head, irritation about the upper lip and nostrils, and a sense of suffocation, so that they could not sleep all night.

"'With these warnings, the mattter now rests with the public.

"'Allow me to remain, sir, yours, &c.,

"THOMAS ORTON.

"'Regent's Terrace, Commercial Road, East, May 14.'"

"If anything could be more startling than the facts you have just quoted," said Mr. Fortescue, after listening with deep attention to the foregoing, "it would be the knowledge that such dangers could be permitted to assail the unwary unchecked. Have no efforts, Chichester, ever been attempted to make the manufacture of such papers penal?"

"You may well ask that question, Fortescue. While popular agitators are incessantly striving to excite the working classes all over England to rise against some imaginary grievance, or to demand some most questionable benefits from the legislature, why will they not take up some real and crying evil such as this? Let them only get up petitions to prohibit the manufacture of poisonous papers, and wreaths, and such like, which is injuring so many of themselves, and their agitation might become a blessing instead of a curse to the country. But in this case, as in many others, beauty is found, when too late, to be a fatal gift; and Englishmen dislike their liberty to be curtailed."

"*Liberty!* But liberty should not degenerate into licence," said Lord Henry, whose attention had been equally aroused. "If we must tamely submit to wholesale poisoning under that plea, one feels inclined to say with Madame Roland, 'O Liberty, what crimes are being committed in thy name!' But surely one would have but to move in the matter, and it would be easy enough to get a bill passed to prohibit the manufacture."

"I earnestly wish you success, Douglass, if you are about to make the attempt. It is said, I know not with what truth, that an effort was made during Lord Palmerston's administration to bring in a measure to that effect, which unhappily failed. I have amongst these extracts a letter from Professor Hoffmann to Mr. Cowper, whose attention, as you will see on reading it, had been directed to the importance of this subject. I think, however, we are now due at the hotel, if my watch is correct, and I had best reserve it for a future occasion."

"You are right, indeed," said Lord Henry. "I had no idea that the time had passed so rapidly. *Allons.*"

CHAPTER VII.

TAUGHT BY EXPERIENCE.

"Experience is a jewel. And it had need be so: for it is often purchased at an infinite rate."
SHAKESPEARE.

Lake of Constance.

"Now," said Lord Henry, as they glided down the Lake of Constance, "these snow-white Alps are inviting us to calm and philosophical contemplation; so seize your opportunity, Chichester, while our minds are imbibing the placidity they infuse. *Revenons à nos moutons*, which means the extracts you were good enough to commence yesterday; that is, if we do not bore you."

"Rather I had feared to weary you," replied his friend. "I have seen so much of the disastrous results of using this green paper on the one hand, and encountered so much prejudice and ridicule when exposing it on the other, that I am not fond of volunteering the information too dearly bought, and too often despised."

"Do not say so," rejoined Lord Henry. "I really hold it a public duty to expose such a record of facts as yours. If we penetrate the dark recesses of a cavern, and find there dank miasmas and poisonous exhalations, common humanity will prompt us to give due warning to those who would otherwise follow in our steps."

"'Take warning by me while you may,' the old song says, and I think you are fully justified in echoing its strains," added Mr. Fortescue; "so now, Chichester, give us some more of your extracts, and we will give you our rapt attention."

"As we are liable to interruptions," returned Sir Robert Chichester, "perhaps the extracts had better give place to some incidents, for the truth of which I can vouch."

"By all means, if you prefer it. Facts as facts are valuable," said Lord Henry.

"Amongst the many instances I have traced of mischief arising from the unsuspected green of the period, I will give you the following," said Sir Robert. "About the time that I was myself suffering in the way I have already described, a house in our neighbourhood was let to some people named Conrad, with whom we had a slight acquaintance. As it happened, this house was also the property of our landlord, and both houses were papered with the same identical paper-hangings."

"And the inmates of course were similarly affected?" interposed Mr. Fortescue.

"Yes; only reversing the order of things," replied Sir Robert. "While I had suffered, my wife had remained unscathed. In the case of our neighbours the arsenic never took the slightest effect on the husband, but produced serious illness in the wife. Mrs. Conrad told me that about a fortnight after they had come into residence, the weather was cold enough for fires in the bedrooms, and from that moment she became perceptibly affected from some cause unknown."

"Did she consult her medical attendant?" asked Lord Henry.

"Yes," replied Sir Robert; "and his visits were continued for months, without any other benefit than very temporary alleviation. In addition to nausea, pain in the eyes, and sore throat, Mrs. Conrad suffered much as I had done from swellings, and threatening of paralysis. Indeed, she lost at times the use of her right hand. Her doctor ordered change of air, and, finding she could not conveniently follow this advice, took his leave, saying he could prescribe no other course, and if she would not go from home she must not again send for him, as he could do no more for her."

"A pleasant state of things truly," said Mr. Fortescue. "And you really attribute her illness to the arsenical paper?"

"I will tell you how the cause was eventually detected," answered Sir Robert. "Mrs. Conrad bore her sufferings as best she could for another fortnight, when, her right arm being powerless, she again ventured to send for her medical man, telling him that medicine must be a sham, and its science a fiction, if it could do nothing to relieve a case like hers. Perhaps this put him on his mettle. At all events he went thoroughly into her case, and then said, 'What coloured paper have you in your bed-room? Will you let me see it?' On being shown upstairs, he remarked that it was certainly a very brilliant green, and as a good deal had been said against such papers, he would test it for her. The following day he sent her word that it contained a very large proportion of arsenic, which would possibly account for her symptoms."

"And the lady wisely banished her green paper, I suppose," said Mr. Fortescue.

"She lost no time in so doing," replied Sir Robert, "and her perplexing and anomalous symptoms ere long disappeared."

"I think you mentioned," observed Lord Henry, "that her husband experienced no evil results."

"None whatever; but a little boy who slept in the dressing-room was never free from inflammatory action of the mouth and throat, and eyes red as if from crying, on awakening in the morning, until the removal of the paper."

"I always observe, if one starts with intent to investigate any given subject," said Mr. Fortescue, "that incidents are constantly recurring which help to elucidate the same, or which assist one in carrying on the inquiry. Upon this principle, Chichester, I doubt not you are for ever picking up facts and observing results regarding this said paper, which would escape the attention of ordinary mortals?"

"I suppose your theory holds good in the present case?" returned Sir Robert, laughing, "for I certainly am always falling foul of the green of the period. I sometimes feel, as it were, a peripatetic lexicon on the subject."

"Rather say an encyclopædia of anecdotes," replied Mr. Fortescue, "for you not only explain your subject, but enliven it with illustrative facts. There is, evidently, an exchange of passengers in preparation at the landing-place we are approaching, but when that feat is achieved, Chichester, do think of something more to tell us."

"I wonder if *la belle Suisse* ever suffers this insidious foe to disturb the peace of travellers," said Lord Henry; "or whether in her innocent simplicity she is as yet unaware of the discovery of Scheele's green."

"You must quit the civilized world, I believe," answered Sir Robert, "before you should cease to be on your guard; that is, if arsenic affects you. In travelling in Switzerland I have not unfrequently had to refuse a bedroom on the same grounds as I did the one you took at Dover. Even at the Hospice of Mount St. Bernard, two or three years ago, the room assigned me harboured my mortal foe, and the monk in charge kindly exchanged it for another which had only wood panelling, and so was unquestionably safe."

"Looking on that glorious snowy range before us," exclaimed Lord Henry, "one cannot believe in any danger from poisoning here, but as we seem all settled again, pray give us some more of your English reminiscences."

"Speaking of avoiding bedrooms on account of their paper-hangings, reminds me of endless adventures in that line, when visiting at friends' houses," said Sir Robert. "Really, susceptibility to arsenical poisoning exposes one's self and one's friends to great trouble, so I do not know that I ought to enlighten you."

"You mean, I suppose, 'where ignorance is bliss, 'tis folly to be wise,'" said Mr. Fortescue. "But your own case, my dear Chichester, proves that ignorance of danger will not suffice to avert its consequences, and I dare say you have been able sometimes to give your friends the clue to illnesses arising from this unsuspected cause."

"Sometimes this has really happened," replied Sir Robert, "and atoned for any annoyance which has arisen through me. Only lately I went to visit a friend who had taken a house for the season at Northton-cum-Mire. The salubrity of the air attracts crowds during the bathing season, and every year the place is becoming fuller. Alas! when shown to my room, I saw bouquets of lilac flowers reposing on the most verdant of green leaves, and about one-fourth of the paper presented 'death on the walls.' It would have been so to me at least, and I had to explain as best I could the awkward fact that I could not sleep there. A second, and a third room was offered me, with like results, and it ended in my having to get a bedroom out of the house. Even this, too, was a service of difficulty, so prone is the fancy of the present day to rest upon this new green."

"Your friends were not a little surprised, I suppose?" said Mr. Fortescue.

"Yes, but they were kind enough to take it very well, and even to express a desire for full information," answered Sir Robert. "In the course of conversation, my friend, Mrs. Beauchamp, suddenly questioned her husband whether green paper could account for the illness of Dr. Scotgur, the leading medical man of the place. I asked the nature of his illness, and learnt that, although not many years established at Northton, Dr. S. was held in the highest estimation, and that there had been a general lamentation among his numerous patients, when, at the beginning of this year, he was seized with low fever which had nearly proved fatal, and had baffled the skill of no fewer than five medical men, some of them from a distance, and of great eminence."

"Did the idea suggest itself to you that his illness arose from arsenical poisoning?" inquired Lord Henry.

"A similarity between his case and my own immediately struck me," replied Sir Robert, "and my suspicions were confirmed on hearing that all his medical advisers agreed in the opinion *that something in the house was poisoning his system.* They had caused the drains to be examined, but could detect nothing which in any wise accounted for his illness. As soon as he could be moved, he was ordered to the Mediterranean, and he had reached Gibraltar before he was able to exert his powers of walking, or even moving without assistance. After remaining abroad for the period pescribed, Dr. S—— had returned with health fully re-established, about a fortnight before the date of my visit. Mrs. Beauchamp added that she had met him a day or two since, and was shocked to see the alteration in his looks since his return. That she had mentioned her fears to another medical man, and his reply was, 'Yes, it is very foolish of him to return to that house; it is evidently something in the house which is poisoning his blood, though we cannot detect the cause of the mischief.'"

"Mrs. Beauchamp, of course, got you to give the doctor the benefit of your experience," remarked Mr. Fortescue.

"Yes; she took me to the house, and though the doctor was out, the 'verdant assassin' was at home, and quickly detected. In the dining-room was a green flock paper, and in the drawing-room a pale green, so we had not far to seek him."

"Did you subsequently see the doctor?"

"Yes, and his sufferings made him open to conviction. It flashed upon him, as it did before upon myself, in the light of a revelation. He said the green paper certainly might account for his strange illness, and that, at all events, he would have it at once removed."

"A sensible man!" remarked Mr. Fortescue, "Have you heard more of him since, Chichester?"

"Yes, in a letter I had lately from Mrs. Beauchamp; she says, 'Dr. Scotgur has had his rooms repapered, and begs me to thank you most warmly for drawing his attention to the subject. He is improved in health, and thinks this may have originated his illness. A curious circumstance I learnt from him. He gives a weekly lecture, which is held in his dining-room. A young lady who lives next door was a regular attendant, and she, too, suffered from low fever at the same time the doctor was prostrated. This was considered confirmatory of the theory that the drains caused both illnesses. She now says she always felt ill after being in Dr. S——'s dining-room, and while there, suffered intensely from smarting of the eyes, &c. So who knows but that your timely visit to Northton, sounding, as you did, the tocsin of war against green paper, may have resulted in a two-fold rescue, and have enlightened very many more on the subject?'"

"I rise to propose a vote of thanks to you, Chichester," said Lord Henry, "for here we are at Romanshorn. I am glad we have just had time for the *finale* of this case, which certainly lends an additional testimony to the irresistible logic of facts."

"I second the vote with all my heart," said Mr. Fortescue, "and hope to hear more on a future occasion."

CHAPTER VIII.

NOBLE INVESTIGATORS.

"Come to " *the workroom* "—to that scene of toil,
Ye intercessors for the child of woe,
Would ye be bearers of the 'wine and oil?'
There let your springs of sympathy o'erflow."
Blighted Pasque Flowers.

Meyringen.

"How splendid a view we have from this window," said Mr. Fortescue, as our three tourists were standing in the *salle à manger* at Meyringen, looking out on the Engelhorner, the Dossenhorn, the Wellhorn, and other mountains, whose snowy peaks were glittering in the sunshine. "We may just as well sit here and enjoy it, Douglass, if we can only get Chichester to while away the time with some more of his instructive revelations."

"They are quite at your service," said Sir Robert Chichester. "I look upon the green of the period, as I have already said, as a verdant assassin, and as such I shall ever most willingly aid in denouncing so mortal a foe. I have also other extracts to show you, which will enable us to view it from another standpoint. Suppose I take you to-day to other workshops than those of the paper-makers, and paper-hangers, where we shall see the same havoc wrought.

"You will remember that Mr. Cowper was led to investigate the subject, and corresponded upon it with Professor Hoffmann in reference to ladies' green wreaths. They are, it seems, coloured with a similar preparation to that used in green papers. The deaths of several of the young women engaged in this poisonous manufacture induced the late Duchess of Sutherland, and the Honourable Mrs. William Cowper, on behalf of the Ladies' Sanitary Association, to write the following letter to the *Times* :—

"'SIR,—Will you allow us to bring under the notice of your readers the melancholy fate of hundreds of young women and children, who, as artificial florists, are suffering in the most terrible manner from handling, and inhaling, the cruelly destructive poison with which they colour the brilliant green leaves now so much the fashion?

"'During their work in the stifling atmosphere necessary for the process, they wrap their faces tightly round with towels, but all precautions are baffled by the subtle character of the light powder, which penetrates the system, producing inflammation and ulceration of the mucous surface of the body. The account in the *Times* about two months ago of the inquest on Matilda Scheurer, who was proved to have been poisoned by emerald green, led us to investigate the subject, and we find that in other instances death has been attributed to the same cause. Some have only escaped her fate by discontinuing the employment for a time. The workers generally dread the occupation, but dread still more the alternative of being without work.

"'We believe that those who, attracted by this gay and brilliant green, risk the danger to themselves of wearing it, will, when they become aware of the suffering occasioned by its preparation, abandon it for a more natural, and, we think, more becoming colour; and we send a statement, kindly made by an eminent professor of chymistry, which we hope may command attention.

"'Your obedient servants,
"'GEORGINA COWPER,
"'ELIZABETH SUTHERLAND.
"'*Secretaries to the Ladies' Sanitary Association.*'

"Then follows the professor's letter, which, I must warn you, is a very long one."

"Not longer than the importance of the subject demands, I'll answer for it," returned Mr. Fortescue. "I am perfectly amazed, Chichester, that hitherto one should have treated it so lightly. Pray give it to us."

"Here it is," replied Sir Robert:—

"'*Royal College of Chymistry, Jan.* 25, 1862.

"'Dear Sir,—In accordance with your wishes, I have examined carefully the green colouring matter of the artificial leaves from a lady's head-dress which you have sent me.

"'It is well known that such leaves generally contain arsenic, and often in considerable quantities. An experienced eye readily recognizes the presence of an arsenic colour (Schweinfurt green) by its brilliancy, the intensity of which is as yet unrivalled by any other green. However, should there remain the slightest doubt, an experiment of the simplest kind would establish the fact. In most cases it would be sufficient to burn such a leaf in order at once to perceive the garlic odour which characterizes the presence of arsenic.

"'In a dozen of the leaves sent me, analysis has

pointed out on an average the presence of 10 grains of white arsenic. I learn from some lady friends that a ball-wreath usually contains about 50 of these leaves. Thus, a lady wears in her hair more than 40 grains of white arsenic, a quantity which, if taken in appropriate doses, would be sufficient to poison 20 persons. This is no exaggeration, for the leaves which you have sent me were, some of them at least, only partly coloured, others only variegated. In consequence of your inquiries, I have been led lately to pay more than usual attention to the head-dresses of ladies, and I observe that the green leaves are often much larger and more deeply coloured than those which I received.

"'The question how far arsenic-dyed wreaths may be prejudicial to health is intimately connected with the discussion, so frequently raised of late years, as to the influence which arsenic-coloured paper-hangings exert upon the human system. This influence has been doubted on various grounds, both by the chemist and the physician. The alleged effect has been attributed to the development of arsenietted hydrogen, or some other volatile arsenic compound, to which the white arsenic, by the action of the damp of the wall, or of the organic constituents of the paper and the paste, might possibly have given rise. Accurate experiments, however often repeated and often varied, have proved the inadmissibility of the assumption of gaseous arsenic exhalations, and, as it so often happens, the injury was denied simply because it could not be explained. Nevertheless, the deleterious effect of arsenic green paper-hangings is at present pretty generally acknowledged. Indeed, it does not require any high-flown hypothesis to explain the transfer of the arsenic from the wall to the system. The arsenic dust, bodily separated from the wall and dispersed over the room, is quite sufficient for this purpose. The investigations of the last few years have clearly shown the presence of arsenic in the dust of rooms hung with arsenic-green paper, even when this dust had been collected at the greatest possible distance from the walls. Moreover, the chronic poisoning by arsenic, of persons living in such rooms has been proved experimentally, inasmuch as the presence of arsenic may be demonstrated in their secretions, more especially if the elimination of the poison be accelerated by the administration of iodide of potassium.

" 'The employment of arsenic green in the manufacture of paper-hangings, in staining paper, in painting children's toys, &c., has attracted the attention of the sanitary authorities on the Continent for many years past. In several of the German States, more particularly in Bavaria, the very country of arsenic colours (which are manufactured on a very large scale in Schweinfurt, a town in Franconia), the application of these colours to papering or painting rooms, has been repeatedly proceeded against. I have before me an edict of the Bavarian Government of the 21st of July, 1845, expressly prohibiting the manufacture and sale of arsenic-green paper-hangings. This general prohibition, it is true, was repealed by an Act of the 23rd of January, 1848, "for industrial considerations," and the use of Schweinfurt green permitted as before for house papering and painting, provided the colour were permanently fixed by appropriate means. The relaxation of the measures against Schweinfurt green appears, however, to have given but little satisfaction. In several papers laid both by chemists and physicians before the Academy of Munich, in its sitting of the 9th of June, 1860, undoubted cases of chronic poisoning produced by arsenic papers, even when glazed, were brought forward, and the

Academy was called upon to represent to the Government the necessity of strictly enforcing the former regulations against arsenic colours, and of removing all Schweinfurt-green wall-colouring from public buildings, schools, hospitals, &c.

"'The immense consumption of arsenic colours, and their reckless use under various conditions prejudicial to health, certainly claim the especial notice and the consideration of the public. Not satisfied with poisoning the wreaths which adorn the heads of our women, modern trade introduces arsenic without scruple even into their dresses. The green tarlatanes so much of late in vogue for ball dresses, according to an analysis made by Professor Erdmann, of Leipsic, contain as much as half their weight of Schweinfurt green. The colour is loosely laid on with starch, and comes off by the slightest friction in clouds of dust. I am told that a ball dress requires about 20 yards of material—an estimate probably below the mark, considering the present fashion. According to the above analysis, these 20 yards would contain about 900 grains of white arsenic. A Berlin physician has satisfied himself that from a dress of this kind no less than 60 grains powdered off in the course of a single evening.

"'It will, I think, be admitted that the arsenic-crowned queen of the ball, whirling along in an arsenic cloud, presents under no circumstances a very attractive object of contemplation; but the spectacle, does it not become truly melancholy when our thoughts turn to the poor poisoned artiste who wove the gay wreath, in the endeavour to prolong a sickly and miserable existence already undermined by this destructive occupation?

"'Ladies cannot, I think, have the remotest idea of the presence of arsenic in their ornaments. If aware of their true nature, they would be satisfied with less brilliant colours; and reject, I have no doubt, these showy green articles, which have not even the merit of being, as far as colouring is concerned, a truthful imitation of nature. There being no longer a demand for them, the manufacture of poisonous wreaths and poisonous dresses would rapidly cease as a matter of course.

"'I remain, dear sir, yours very sincerely,

"'A. W. HOFFMANN.

"''To the Right Hon. William Cowper, &c.'"

"Would that the demand might cease," exclaimed Mr. Fortescue, "if thus only this abominable traffic is to be extirpated. Well, Douglass, I think the least return we can make to Chichester is to pledge ourselves to go heart and soul into the subject, and to run, if needful, the gauntlet of badinage in our efforts to ventilate the subject."

"Indeed, I think we can no longer plead ignorance, or indulge in apathy with a safe conscience," returned Lord Henry. "I now remember reading in the papers a few months ago an account of two young ladies who appeared at a ball in green tarlatan dresses. Did you notice it, Fortescue?"

"No; what caused the mention of their dresses?" asked Mr. Fortescue.

"Why, as soon as they began to dance, clouds of green dust were seen, and in the midst of a waltz a young officer, the unfortunate partner of one of them, fell down in a state of insensibility, and was carried out apparently dead."

"I wonder if they knew the danger they incurred, as well as the pests they rendered themselves in society," said Mr. Fortescue.

"Pride suffers no pain, and fashion cannot pause to be merciful," returned Lord Henry. "But, Chichester, I see you have some other extracts. Do they bear on the same subject?"

"Yes; but as you have proved yourselves such reflecting students, I think you deserve to be let out of school. We really must not waste this glorious morning by remaining any longer indoors."

CHAPTER IX.

THE LOGIC OF FACTS.

> "With impotence of will
> We wheel, tho' ghastly shadows interpose,
> Round us, and round each other."—*Shelley.*

Under the Jungfrau.

"It is almost a sin to yawn in the presence of that majestic Jungfrau," said Lord Henry, the day after their arrival at Interlachen; "but what is a fellow to do? I have spelt through the *Times*, having previously made a mental vow to cast politics to the winds, and I have walked over to the window at least a dozen times an hour to see if there is any chance of its clearing up; but rain, rain, rain seems the order of the day, and however one may rave over *la neige éternelle*, the most poetic mind can see nothing in this *pluie éternelle.*"

"Then you never took your degree in Longfellow?"

said Mr. Fortescue, "or 'Be still, sad heart, and cease repining' would rebuke your impatience. Not but what I am as provoked as you are at this *contretemps*. What shall we do to amuse ourselves?"

"Why, call upon Chichester, of course, for some of his wonderful stories in proof of the danger of civilized life. I say, old fellow, can't you put down your book, and enliven us once more with some tale of horrors, real or imaginary, arising from the use of green paper? I'm quite a convert, by the way, and when I marry I intend to stipulate that my wife should hold your views on the subject as an article of faith."

"The Lord Henry Douglass is pleased to be facetious, and is so evidently orthodox on the subject that we may assume the Lady Henry will share his intelligent convictions," said Sir Robert Chichester, looking up from his book. "But even on a rainy day I cannot be a penny-a-liner; and one thing I must premise, that neither in the past, present, or future have I drawn, nor will I draw, upon a lively imagination for one single fact, which I state for the purpose of enlightening you."

"Pardon my nonsense; in this inspiring air one's spirits are ever ready to rise like a cork in a bottle of champagne. But, now, I am really all anxiety for further information and instruction," said Lord Henry.

"Fortescue, do you remember our old friend, Mrs. Mackenzie?" asked Sir Robert. "You used to know her well as Miss Blair; in fact, I am not sure there was not some tender sentiment on your part."

"I remember her well as Miss Blair, and a beautiful girl she was. But soon after her marriage her husband's regiment was ordered out to India, and since then I have lost sight of her. Have you seen her lately, Chichester?"

"I found myself some time ago in the neighbourhood of Easton," replied Sir Robert, "and determined to call. Curious to say, it is Henry Douglass' thirst for knowledge which at this moment recalls that visit to my remembrance."

"Why, was Mrs. Mackenzie one of your converts?" asked Mr. Fortescue.

"Not one of mine," said Sir Robert. "I found her fully awakened to the importance of the subject, by a process somewhat similar to that which had quickened my own apprehensions of it. In other words, she told me she had been very ill, and had been almost given over from the self-same cause."

"Indeed! I suppose you compared notes?" remarked Mr. Fortescue.

"We did so," replied Sir Robert. "Their drawing-room had been recently hung with a very pretty soft-coloured green paper. At that time Mrs. Mackenzie said she was in perfect health, but shortly after the room had been repapered she began to experience some strange sensations. I need not recapitulate them. I give you both credit for being sufficiently apt scholars to know the symptoms of arsenical poisoning by this time almost as well as I do myself. The doctor never suggested, or suspected the cause of her illness; indeed, in all my researches, which, as you may believe, are by this time tolerably extensive, I have rarely heard of one who did so of his own accord. I could multiply instances in which their patients have died before the cause was discovered, and I could fill a volume with cases in which these enlightened *savans* have treated the idea with open ridicule, or silent contempt; but our poor friend's case is only one of thousands in which the poison has been permitted to undermine the constitution undisturbed by the Faculty, till a state of chronic, if not morbid, irritation has set in."

"Then how was the discovery made at last?" asked Lord Henry.

"As in nine cases out of ten, almost accidentally," replied Sir Robert. "When she had become alarmingly ill, and no relief seemed likely to be obtained, it suddenly occurred to her servants to mention a fact connected with the papering of the drawing-room. They remembered when the men were employed in hanging this paper, they used frequently to come into the kitchen complaining of faintness and sickness, which, they said, was caused by the green paper. They further remembered, when the paper-hangers had nearly completed their work, that on one occasion they had remarked that only one of the men had gone home to his dinner. Wondering what had occurred to detain his fellow-workman, they went into the room, when they were startled by seeing him sitting on the floor, bent almost double, his head resting on his knees. In answer to their inquiry if he was ill, he roused himself sufficiently to whisper slowly, and with difficulty, 'Get me out of this room.' Believing that a fit of some sort had seized him, they assisted him into the open air, and, as soon as he could speak, his first words were, 'You have saved my life! If I had stayed ten minutes longer in that room I think I should have died.'"

"Was the man, then, aware of the danger you have told us of?" asked Mr. Fortescue.

"Fully," replied Sir Robert, "and every paperhanger in the trade, as I have ascertained by careful inquiry, is so."

"It is almost unaccountable, if such is the case, that such papers are made," remarked Lord Henry.

"We will discuss that question anon," said Sir Robert Chichester. "Meanwhile I will finish the story. To the servants the man's assertions were, of course, Greek, and they naturally inquired what was the matter with the room? 'Oh, it is that green paper,' he replied. 'It is poisonous, and we none of us can work at it for more than two days together. Some of us can only be employed upon it one day in a fortnight. I was so anxious to get my part of the work done, that I thought I would stay on extra time, but it was very foolish of me, and I have been properly punished.' This incident duly furnished a nine days' wonder in the servants' hall, but regarding it as an idiosyncrasy, their sagacity failed to perceive a principle, or work out a theory, and poor Mrs. Mackenzie paid the penalty of their want of apprehension."

"The obnoxious paper had, of course, been

discarded before the date of your visit?" remarked Mr. Fortescue.

"They had had it varnished over," replied Sir Robert, "which they had been assured would answer every purpose. But Mrs. Mackenzie told me she sometimes thought the evil was not quite cured, and regretted that they had not taken it down."

"How passing strange that the servants did not at once allude to the peril, which in this case was so apparent," said Mr. Fortescue.

"As regards the poor man, it certainly was so," said Sir Robert, "but I can quite understand that even in his case the cause and effect would scarcely connect themselves in their profound minds. And as for the probability that other people would be similarly affected in the same room, it would, of course, never cross their imaginations."

"And I fancy you think their betters are equally obtuse?" remarked Mr. Fortescue.

"*On juge par soi*," returned his friend. "I confess I had heard of cases before my own illness which ought to have opened my eyes, but somehow I never reduced these facts to a theory, and (though now it seems unaccountable) never dreamt of their having any application to myself."

"I remember one such instance in particular," continued Sir Robert, "though at the time it made not the slightest impression upon me. You know my uncle's place, Youlcliff, Fortescue? Well, a few years ago the large dining-room required re-papering, and a green flock was selected. The first day it was used, my uncle was taken suddenly ill at dinner. The next day the same thing occurred, and again the third day, when, thinking the poor old baronet required change, they left home for a short tour. Curious to say, upon his return the strange symptoms re-appeared. Without analyzing the cause, they dined for some days in the smaller dining-room, until his health seemed quite re-established. The arrival of company made them dine once more under the upas tree, so to speak, and as my poor uncle was again led from the room, one of the company suggested the arsenical paper as the would-be assassin. It was immediately analyzed, and the arsenic detected. The paper was taken down, and from that day to this I have heard of no similar attacks."

"Certainly conclusive evidence enough," said Mr. Fortescue; "but returning for a moment to Mrs. Mackenzie's case, let me ask if her husband suffered at all?"

"Yes; in his case it brought on weakness of the walls of the heart, as his medical man called it, and he was ordered off to Italy in consequence."

"Well, Chichester, your stories are most convincing, and worth any money, especially on a wet day," said Lord Henry. "But I am sure you will sympathize in my present satisfaction, when I announce that the rain has meanwhile ceased, and that we shall just have time to climb the Heimwelfluh, and feast our eyes upon the Mönch, the Eiger, the Silberhorn, and the Jungfrau, before the bell summons us to the table d'hôte."

CHAPTER X.

FURTHER REVELATIONS.

"'Twere long to tell, and sad to trace
    Each step . . . ."

Grindelwald.

"Well, I think we have done our duty to-day, if not to society in general, at least to ourselves in particular," exclaimed Lord Henry Douglass. "I say, Fortescue and Chichester, are you up to another walk across the Wengern Alp?"

"Not to-night exactly," returned Mr. Fortescue. "Indeed, I think we shall all require a day or two to recruit, after this pedestrian feat, which I suppose the Alpine Club would regard in the light of child's play. To say the truth, Grindelwald is far more to my taste than Interlachen, which you, Douglass, found so inspiring; so, a halt here will be by no mean disagreeable to me."

"I quite agree with you, Fortescue, in your comparative estimate of Grindelwald," said Sir Robert, "although my last remembrance of the place is connected with terrible sufferings."

"Why, were you laid up here?" inquired both his friends.

"Not precisely laid up," returned Sir Robert, "but I was a martyr to neuralgia, or tic-douloureux in the face at that time, and it seemed to reach its climax at this very hotel. Day after day I had to leave the table d'hôte, and well do I remember rolling on the ground almost in convulsions, so great was the agony I had to endure."

"I almost wonder you ventured to come here again," said Mr. Fortescue.

"The place was not to blame," said Sir Robert; "and now the cause is, I am thankful to say, removed; so I hope to explore and enjoy Grindelwald more than on the former occasion, when I could not venture across either of its glaciers."

"Now, was green paper, *par hasard*, the delinquent in that case?" inquired Mr. Fortescue.

"I believe it was, though I had no suspicion of it at the time. I mentioned neuralgia, if you remember, amongst the many symptoms of the poisoning to which I was subjected, but when the cause was detected and removed, this symptom obstinately refused to disappear. It must have been two or three years after the arsenical discovery, before we made the tour which brought us to this place; and during all that time I could never count upon entire freedom from tic. The agony I thus endured was shattering the nervous system to such an extent that Dr. C——, of Paris, apprehended consequences worse than death, and assured my friends that prolonged travel afforded me the only chance of saving life and reason. And the leading dentist in Paris declined the responsibility of the experiment which I wished him to make, which was, to see if tooth extraction could relieve the pain."

"You returned to London in this sad plight?" inquired Lord Henry.

"I returned to London, and consulted a dentist who has made sympathetic affections in connexion with our dental plagues his special study," answered Sir Robert. "He decided on removing three of my grinders, and attached to the roots, in each case, was a substance as large as a pea; indeed, in the case of one, it was double the size. The dentist assured me that mischief far less extensive had often caused paralysis, and in some instances had produced insanity and even death."

"But was this likewise attributed to green paper?" asked Mr. Fortescue

"I asked Winterton this question," replied Sir Robert, "and was assured by him that if I were a subject liable to be affected by arsenic, it was precisely the effect which might be expected."

"Could you trace back the origin of your tic, as you had endured this martyrdom for years?" inquired Lord Henry.

"I could, distinctly," answered Sir Robert. "Immediately after I first had a study papered with green paper, this frightful neuralgia began. But enough of oneself. I was going to impart the information I gleaned from my dentist."

"Had he known of similar cases?" asked Lord Henry.

"It was more in regard to the action of arsenic that I questioned him. Winterton told me that the American dentists employed this agency largely for destroying the nerve before stopping a tooth, and that its action is almost instantaneous. But, he added, the mischief sometimes caused by it was so fearful, that he would not consent to employ it, or encounter the risk."

"To what mischief did he allude?" asked Mr. Fortescue.

"I asked the same question," said Sir Robert. "He said, 'The arsenic enters into, and becomes absorbed in the system immediately. It is impossible to foresee what after-results may follow, as so much depends upon the physical state of the patients.' Winterton, however, assured me that he had frequently known tumours and fungus at the roots of the tooth, caused by the application of arsenic. You will not, therefore, wonder that in my own case, I at once coupled cause and effect together."

"Well, one must confess they are not unequally yoked," said Lord Henry. "What between green dresses, green leaves, and green paper, however, it seems that we are encompassed with dangers of which one has not the slightest conception till one falls in with a *savan* like you, Chichester. I really intend to enlighten all my friends when I go home; so tell us as much as you can. Your extracts are not exhausted yet, if I remember right. Can you make another dip into them?"

"Yes; here is another which I lately cut out of one of the daily papers," replied Sir Robert, "headed 'The Shocking Death of a Girl from sucking Artificial Flowers.' It is a report of the coroner's inquest, respecting the death of Elizabeth Anne Abdalla, a girl aged fourteen years, who was shown to have died from the effects of sucking an artificial grape. I will give it you verbatim :—

"'It will be recollected, from the evidence given on the previous occasion, that the deceased was on Sunday, the 25th September, taken suddenly ill with pains and cramps in the stomach, and died the next morning. The mother of the deceased stated that her daughter and another girl had been out walking together, and that the other girl had given deceased some artificial flowers which she had been made a present of by her mistress, who was a milliner. The deceased, her playmate said, sucked only one green artificial grape. After death, Mr. Chandler, M.R.C.S., made a post-mortem examination, and found that the coatings of the stomach were ulcerated, and that there were traces of an irritant poison. The inquiry had been adjourned for the purpose of getting Dr. Letheby to make an analysis of the contents of the stomach, and also the artificial flowers.

"'Dr. Letheby said that he had made an analysis of the contents of the stomach, and found that the liver contained arsenic to the amount of three grains. The colouring matter of the artificial leaves and grapes was analyzed. The blue and pink kinds contained no poison, *but the green ones were covered with arsenical green, arsenite of copper.* Ten grapes contained three grains of poison. He produced a specimen of the metallic arsenic obtained from a single grape. The artificial leaves are also stained with arsenical green. *Each leaf contains about a grain and a half of poison.* The quantity of poison contained in a leaf was, perhaps, sufficient to kill a child. He had heard from Mr. Chandler a statement of the case, and he (Dr. Letheby) attributed deceased's death to poison.

"'In November, 1861, Dr. Letheby heard of a similar instance—two children who kept their toys in a cupboard lined with green paper. Both were taken very ill, and one died. Upon making analysis of the paper, he found six inches of it to contain 13 grains of arsenic—a quantity sufficient to kill two persons. There are a number of different kinds of green sold; they contain from 58 to 71 per cent. of arsenic. In many cases the green colour is mixed with chalk and plaster of Paris, *to lower the depth of the colour.* Arsenical green is used for paper toys, artificial flowers, and even for ladies' dresses. A wreath of fifty green leaves contains enough to kill ten men; and a green tarlatan dress, 20 yards, contained 900 grains of arsenic. He had heard of several cases of this description, and thought that the public ought to take some precaution against them.

"'The jury, after some deliberation, returned the following verdict: "That the death of the deceased, Elizabeth Anne Abdalla, was caused through inadvertently sucking artificial grapes, which contained arsenite of copper." *The jury expressed a hope that some measure would be brought in to prevent the use of arsenic as a colour.*'"

"You promised to enlighten us, Chichester, before our tour was over," said Mr. Fortescue, "and I must confess after this, if we poison either ourselves or our friends by arsenical paper-hangings, we can never again urge ignorance in extenuation. Do tell me, as you must have startled many others with the same facts, whether you have generally found people open to conviction or not?"

"And whether their convictions have gone to the extent of pulling down their obnoxious papers or not?" added Lord Henry.

"It takes a long time, in most things, to convince

people against their will," answered their friend. "I have observed this, that if people do yield an intelligent assent to the said facts, and act upon the same, they do so at once, or their alarm soon subsides, and, even if illness follows upon neglect of the warning, they are seldom aroused a second time.

"I remember once visiting a friend in Derbyshire, and so reasonable did the note of alarm appear to him, when once he had heard the facts, and weighed the evidence, that he set off for London the following week, and chose new papers for at least eight of his rooms. Others adopt half-measures. One man, for instance, on hearing my story, was so alarmed at the reflection that his own bedroom and dressing-room were papered with a virulent arsenical green, that he went to the extent of repapering the former, but there he stopped. No persuasions would induce him to repaper his dressing-room, though he has often suffered from some of the symptoms of arsenical poisoning. Other friends have been seemingly aroused at first, but, on subsequent visits, I have found the green of the period as lively as ever, and some one or more of the family paying the penalty of neglect in their health, while their minds had subsided into apathy and scepticism on the subject.".

"I am sure, my dear Chichester," said Lord Henry, "you will have the satisfaction of seeing that both Fortescue and myself are fully alive to a sense of the peril we have unknowingly incurred. Indeed, the fact of my having kept awake this evening, after the exertions of the pedestrian feat we have achieved, is conclusive evidence in my favour. But nature has its limits, and I for one must now rest in the arms of Morpheus."

CHAPTER XI.

A MATHEMATICAL DEMONSTRATION.

> "You turn, and turn, and turn again,
> To solve the mystery, but in vain;
> Stand still and breathe, and take from me,
> A clue that soon shall set you free."
>
> "Je noterai cela Madame, dans mon livre."
> Molière.

Lucerne.

"I VOTE for spending some days at Lucerne," said Lord Henry Douglass, the evening of their arrival. "After alpen-stocking it from Grindelwald over the Furka Pass to Hospenthal, and descending the St. Gotthard *à pied* to the Lake of the Four Cantons, a fellow may be excused if he indulges in the *dolce far niente* mood on reaching the Schweitzerhof."

"With all my heart," said Mr. Fortescue, "especially as there are several mild excursions within reach. There is the Righi to be done; and Mount

Pilatus, which last, some think, presents the most graceful outline in Switzerland."

"And, independently of the foregoing consideration, I willingly vote with the majority on the present occasion," said Sir Robert Chichester, "for I directed my letters to be sent here, and it does not appear as if they had yet arrived; so the ayes have it."

"I found a letter from my wife on arriving, just now," said Mr. Fortescue; "and, by the bye, there is a message to you, Chichester, in it. Mrs. Fortescue is spending some time, during my absence, with some old friends—Sir George and Lady Furlong—in Wales, and I have told her of your grand discoveries on a certain point, and now I must refer to her letter for some inquiries she wishes me to make.

"Oh, this is it!" he continued. "It seems that Llangwellan Castle has been lately repapered, while the Furlongs were abroad, and even since their return, poor Sir George has been constantly complaining of his throat. Indeed, not long ago he seems to have had ulceration to such an extent that they were quite alarmed, and had Dangerfield, the great surgeon, down from London. Mrs. Fortescue wants me to ask you if you think green paper can have anything to do with it."

"The nerves of the face and throat are precisely the parts which are usually first affected by arsenic," replied Sir Robert, "and ulceration of the throat is, as we have seen, one of the most ordinary symptoms; but I did not clearly understand that your friends had chosen that colour in their recent paperings."

"Oh, no! I am telling my story by halves. Mrs. Fortescue says she read my letter to Lady Furlong, and asked if that could be the cause of her husband's illness. Lady Furlong said the same suggestion had been made by others, but she did not think there could be any ground for such a fear. They agreed to go and examine the paper, and here is her report:—

"'The paper is a very pretty one, and certainly has no green in the grounding. But it is a mass of bouquets of flowers, and consequently green leaves are there by the thousand, of a brilliant colour, such as I conclude, by what you tell me, can only be obtained by arsenic. The question I wish you would ask Sir Robert Chichester is, whether this can possibly account for poor Sir George's frequent throat affections? Lady Furlong says, even if so small a quantity could produce any prejudicial effects, nothing of the sort has ever affected her husband; but we both await your reply.'"

"I have the highest opinion of the tact, energy, and perseverance of ladies in any cause they advocate, and I only hope, if Mrs. Fortescue attempts to warn her friends of the danger that lurks in the green of the period, her powers of persuasion may be equal to her discernment. But tell her she has undertaken a very difficult task, as I know by long experience. I must not make her a coward, or, I would add, it is one which I would gladly resign into her hands."

"Then you really attribute our friend's illness to arsenical poisoning?" asked Mr. Fortescue.

"Oh, that would be taking a leap in the dark," said Sir Robert, "without far more grounds for forming a judgment than I at present possess. Personal experience in my own case was so decisive and so dearly purchased, that one fears lest one should be tempted to ride one's hobby to death. I would only suggest that some of the cases you have heard should be laid before your friends, and then, perhaps, if Sir George's illness recurs, they may think it advisable to change the paper, or the room by way of an experiment. For myself, I always now avoid trifling with known poisons."

"I suppose," remarked Mr. Fortescue, "it is quite possible that when there is a tendency to throat affection, the pernicious effects of the arsenical papers would be immediately felt, though previously they may have exerted no injurious influence?"

"Precisely so," responded Sir Robert; "and as an eel gets used to skinning, it is quite possible that, with a strong constitution, a man may successfully resist the effects of arsenic after struggling awhile under its influence. But is it worth the struggle? Life is too short, and health too precious, to run needless risks; and what is the use of sacrificing either to an idea?"

"But surely a few small leaves interspersed amongst flowers can do no great damage, even admitting the virulence of the poison," said Lord Henry.

"Yet salt water would be equally saline, whether taken up in a hogshead or in a wine glass," remarked Mr. Fortescue.

"I lately met your argument, Douglass," replied Sir Robert Chichester, "when trying to convince a friend, by getting him to compute the number of such leaves in his own room. In each column of the pattern there were about a hundred little green leaves; and as there were altogether a hundred such columns round the room, it resulted that he was perpetually inhaling the dust given off by ten thousand spots of arsenic, averaging the size of a sixpence, each containing perhaps a grain of poison. This is easily calculated, but no one has yet been able to ascertain how infinitesimal may be the dose which will powerfully affect our visual, aural, or olfactory nerves, nor how subtily poisons, and even odours, may act upon the system."

"You are quite right there," returned Lord Henry. "I remember once a train of similarly philosophical reflections being started in my own mind, struck by a single match."

"Metaphorically?" inquired Mr. Fortescue.

"No! a *bond fide* lucifer, which being struck in my father's hall, instantly filled the whole vestibule with its intolerable odour. I tried to calculate the proportion between the atom of brimstone employed, and the immense space in which the air was vitiated, but it was utterly beyond my arithmetical powers. The weight of the sulphur could not have been half a grain, yet, had a thousand persons been present, each would have been sensibly affected by the odour diffused. I moralized and philosophized over these facts, thinking how impossible it was accurately to circumscribe the limits or to define the nature of infection."

"Worthy of Hahnemann himself, Douglass!" exclaimed Mr. Fortescue; "but I declare I can cap your philosophy by repeating a piece of information given me by Hendrick the last time I consulted him. He was alluding to some recent poisoning case, and stating how long different substances could remain in the system, which led him to mention this fact amongst others. He said that a grain of musk might be exposed in a room for fifty, or even a hundred years, the whole of that time diffusing a strong perfume, and yet at the end of the century, if tested, no appreciable diminution would have taken place in the weight, or scent."

"You have at least added the weight of a most interesting fact to the subject we have in hand," said Sir Robert Chichester. "Did Dr. Hendrick proceed to apply it?"

"We did not discuss green paper," replied Mr. Fortescue, "but I remember he instanced arsenic and strychnine, each of which, he said, might be exposed to the action of time and climate, and a grain would remain a grain, full weight, when a hundred years had passed away. Speaking of strychnine, the poison employed on this occasion, he quoted the opinion of Herepath, as given in his evidence on the inquest. This great authority asserted that strychnine, when received into the system, undergoes no change, and after it has done its deadly work, the precise amount taken will be found in the body, unimpaired as to weight or efficiency. *Ergo*, that were it to be re-administered to a fresh victim each time it had completed its previous mission, *one grain would suffice to extirpate the whole human race!*"

"We are not yet sufficiently alive to the potency of poisons," returned his friend; "but apply all this to our green papers, admitted, as they are by every honest paper-manufacturer, to be produced by arsenic. Assume, for the nonce, that you want to kill your visitor by arsenic. It must be in one of two ways; by its physical action, or by its chemical. If you employ the former you must get a block of arsenic, and use it as you would a brickbat. If the latter, you must dissolve or dilute the arsenic in air or water, or some agency which will hold, it and thus convey it into his system. Now it is just this which is ready done for you in all papers in which 'Scheele's green,' the green of the period, mind you, is used.

"When we get home," continued Sir Robert, "if you

can put your hand on some old numbers of *Chambers' Journal*, you will find a capital story built on this very fact, of an uncle who is supposed to wish to rid himself of a young heir who stands in his light."

"Indeed; have you any notion in what number this appears?" inquired Lord Henry.

"My pocket-book, I believe, will tell you," answered Sir Robert, referring to it. "Yes, it is Number 454, and appeared in September, 1862."

"But perhaps the heir's room was all green," suggested Mr. Fortescue.

"True, but the greater includes the less, as we but lately agreed," replied his friend; "and the bite of the asp may be as fatal as that of the rattlesnake."

"To return to my wife's letter, and her inquiry respecting papers such as she found at Llangwellan," said Mr. Fortescue, "I gather that you would avoid sleeping in a room with never so small a proportion of green in the paper. Am I right?"

"I must confess to the disagreeable fact, as far as I am personally concerned," replied Sir Robert, "and that I would advise a similar course to any who may have become equally susceptible to the action of arsenic. A simile will best explain the reason why. The clouds of dust we encountered in descending the St. Gotthard this morning passed by and left us unscathed; but the same dust might have reawakened serious inflammation of the eyes in the case of one who had but recently recovered from such a malady. Those who, like myself, have but just escaped the jaws of death through the action of arsenical dust, will soon learn, to their cost, that they at least, dare not trifle with the poison."

"Well, I hope you have examined your bedroom paper, Fortescue, as I can answer for it Chichester has his," said Lord Henry; "we really must adjourn the debate, interesting and philosophic though it be, and try to sleep over all we have heard. *Bon soir!*"

CHAPTER XII.

ANOTHER VICTIM.

"Evil is wrought by want of thought,
As well as want of heart."

On the Linden.

"FORTESCUE seems to have given us the slip this morning," said Lord Henry, as he strolled into the *salle à manger*. "I can nowhere find him."

"Nor I either," returned Sir Robert Chichester, "but the *garçon* told me Monsieur had gone out early with a friend, and had left word for us not to wait for him if he were late in returning."

The mountain air had braced up the walking powers of the absentee; so, at least, his friends agreed, when, having dispatched their breakfast, they set off for the Linden, *viá* the Lion, on the overhanging heights, to await his return.

"Now, Douglass, admire the view," said Sir

Robert, "I sometimes am tempted to think it the grandest in all Switzerland."

"It is nothing short of magnificent," returned his friend, "with the Righi on our left, and Mount Pilatus just unveiling his stern head on our right, and that unrivalled chain of semicircling Alps which unite the two, what can one desire more of grandeur, sublimity, and beauty."

"The surroundings of the Lake of Lucerne are acknowledged, I believe," said Sir Robert, "to be the grandest in mountain scenery, and the route we have taken prepares us to recognize the opposite chain almost as old acquaintances."

"Yes, and here comes another old acquaintance, if I mistake not," replied Lord Henry, "but who can Fortescue have picked up?"

Mr. Fortescue, for it was himself, soon came up to them, and introduced the Rev. Percy Herbert, as a friend with whom he had had an unexpected rencontre.

"The beauty of the morning tempted me out before either of you were astir," explained Mr. Fortescue, in answer to their inquiries, "and who should I see standing at the door of the hotel but my old friend Herbert. I proposed, and he seconded, a walk to the Little Righi, which, we were told, would occupy us only fifty minutes, but the view was superb, and I suppose we lingered too long."

"Are you making an extensive tour in Switzerland?" said Lord Henry, addressing Mr. Herbert.

"Not very extensive. I know Switzerland well; but at present I am travelling more for health than for prolonged enjoyment, and the air here, with its mountain breezes, is a grand restorative."

"And, Douglass, won't Chichester be charmed when he hears that my friend's illness has been caused by green paper?" said Mr. Fortescue.

"You rank me as a Nero then, and think I delight in the sufferings of my species?" inquired Sir Robert Chichester.

"No, indeed, not that," exclaimed Mr. Fortescue, "I only meant that I had brought you an unexpected ally, who will back you up in all you say against the green of the period."

"I assure you I shall gladly hear Mr. Herbert's testimony, which will doubtless corroborate all I have told you," said Sir Robert. "Have you long been a sufferer from this poison?"

"Yes; indeed I would ostracize all the green paper that is made," replied Mr. Herbert, "not merely for the sufferings it has inflicted on myself, but from the almost daily ravages I find it making amongst my friends and parishioners. I was mentioning to Fortescue some of the instances which constantly come under my notice, and he told me you had likewise had pretty extensive experiences in its ill-effects."

"My friends here can tell you that the results of my experience have been largely inflicted upon them," said Sir Robert, "but *una voce poco fà;* and a second witness will be most valuable."

"Your parish is a very large one in London, is it not, Herbert?" asked Mr. Fortescue.

"Yes, and with a rapidly increasing population," answered Mr. Herbert. "When you come and pay me a visit I will show you whole streets which have sprung up since I came to it. In one of these, containing about fifty small houses, I remember making a special note in my journal, to the effect that in each house there was more or less of green paper; and subsequently entering the remarkable fact, that in every one of those dwellings there was sickness, and occasionally death, before even the first twelvemonth was over.

"Even in a model lodging-house in my parish," continued Mr. Herbert, "where the rooms are let out in sets, there is scarcely a single set where the green of the period may not be seen in some form or other, in one or more of the rooms. With many of the families inhabiting them, sore throats and other symptoms appear chronic. The inmates are alive to the danger, but ask what can they do? They cannot afford to repaper, and the company to whom it belongs laugh at the idea."

"You endeavour at least to enlighten your parishioners?" said Sir Robert.

"Yes; and having suffered from this noxious poison, I am naturally on the *qui vive* in every house I enter, for my own sake, lest I should be requested to inhale an arsenical atmosphere. And when once one's wits are sharpened on the subject, you have no conception how constantly you come in contact with it."

"So my friend Chichester tells us," returned Mr. Fortescue. "I dare say you have a portfolio of anecdotes which would vie with his."

"I could tell you instances by scores, if you have any curiosity to hear them," replied Mr. Herbert. "A few months since, a gentleman called on me, and begged me to come and visit his wife, who was extremely ill, and very anxious and nervous about herself. They had come into my parish two years previously. Until that period his wife had been in perfect health, and of a happy, cheerful disposition. Her illness began on taking possession of their new house, and had gradually increased till both mind and body seemed giving way. The symptoms mentioned were general debility, loss of appetite, failing eyesight, and inability to read much. She had had partial paralysis of the hand and arm, and at times was unable to lift her foot from the ground. Together with all this, she suffered much from mental depression."

"And you conceive green paper to have originated her illness?" asked Mr. Fortescue.

"The foregoing was told me before I saw the lady herself," said Mr. Herbert. "On entering her room, I perceived at once both cause and effect in the arsenical paper which surrounded her, and in the distressed look, and irritable state in which I found her. On further questioning her husband, I learnt that since she had occupied that poisoned room, she had suffered from diphtheria, and that on one occasion, when she went to consult Dr. Ramston, he said, 'What have you been doing? Your blood is poisoned.' The verdant paper was not, however, suspected, until the date of my visit, and

I shall not soon forget the gratitude of the poor husband when I told him the probable cause and remedy."

" May I ask what remedy you suggested ?" asked Sir Robert.

" The first was to remove her into another room, free from any signs of green, which they did that very evening, and on my visit next day I learnt that she had passed a better night than she had for months. I then advised that she should try a course of Caplin's Electro-Chemical Baths, which in my own case had been effectual in drawing the poison from the system. She followed my advice in every particular, and I have since had the great pleasure of witnessing her gradual restoration to health and happiness."

" How grateful her family must be to you," said Lord Henry.

"They have, indeed, expressed themselves most warmly," said Mr. Herbert. " Her husband felt matters had come to an extremity. No doctoring did her good. She, who had been a devoted mother, could scarcely bear the sight of her children; even to him she had become cold and impatient; all her friends remarked, and grieved at the strange change which had passed over her. It was thus an unspeakable relief to be assured that there was a physical and palpable cause at work, but far more so to learn that the cause was one with which they could grapple—and then the joy with which they saw her restored to her natural state can be better imagined than described."

"Do you find all your parishioners equally amenable to reason?" inquired his friend.

"Far from it. I can recall at this moment a house where the drawing-room paper has a green ground, and where all the bedrooms occupied by the family have still brighter greens. The mother is always ailing, and in the doctor's hands. From time to time she has serious illnesses, and is given over—arsenic being all the time written on the countenance. The only daughter is almost as delicate, and is frequently suffering from either diphtheria, or English cholera, being laid up sometimes for months together. I have warned and urged them again and again, and, much to their doctor's credit, he has also hinted that the paper is not quite safe; but they plead the expense of its removal, and so the paper remains, and the mischief continues, and will to the end of the chapter."

"Herbert, you and my friend Chichester were born to run in a curricle," said Mr. Fortescue. "We must hear some more of your reminiscences; but it is getting hot up here. Let us seek the shade of the grove lower down; and perhaps you will go on with your graphic details."

CHAPTER XIII.

THE VERDICT.

> "I'll read you matter deep and dangerous;
> As full of peril, and adventurous spirit,
> As to o'erwalk a current roaring loud
> On the unsteadfast footing of a spear."
>
> *King Henry IV.*

Lake of the Four Cantons.

"MAY I ask," said Lord Henry, when they had established themselves in more shady quarters, "why you mentioned the doctor's hint as being so greatly to his credit? If I may venture to say so, I should have thought it more in his line than yours to trace the cause and origin of diseases."

"You are, doubtless, right in theory, my lord," said Mr. Herbert; "but, in fact, medical men, as a body, are not wholly free from prejudice and bigotry. Such, at least, has been my experience, though I have met with some noble exceptions.

Dr. Llaughton, for one, is most persevering in trying to arouse the attention of his patients to the danger they are perpetually incurring from inhaling a poisoned atmosphere. I once mentioned to him the opposition I had met with from medical men; for when I have convinced my people of the cause of some mysterious illness, and the paper appears doomed, I hear, on my next visit, that they have mentioned it to Dr. So-and-so, and 'he quite laughed at the idea of the paper doing them any harm.'"

"And what did Llaughton say?" asked Lord Henry.

"He said, 'Even if they are convinced, you cannot expect them to urge the consideration of the subject too strongly. Don't you know that many medical men look upon a case of hysteria as an annuity?'"

"Which inspired, I suppose, the poet's muse," interposed Lord Henry, "when he wrote—

"'Fools are their bankers—a prolific line,
And every mortal malady's a mine.'"

"And, apart from the frailty of human nature, under which head we must deposit that last fact," said Sir Robert Chichester, "the blindness one sometimes meets with, in quarters where one would least expect it, is amazing. Fortescue, do you remember our both consulting Dr. Millrod, some years ago?"

"Yes, I do. What has become of him?"

"He has taken up his abode at one of our English watering-places; and, being lately in his neighbourhood, I paid him a visit. He showed me over his establishment, where all seemed flourishing, and into a large hall, which he was about to repaper. He unrolled a piece of the intended decorations, and, lo and behold, a beautiful tint of arsenical green!"

"The Doctor was, then, unaware of the danger?" remarked Mr. Fortescue.

"Not at all," rejoined Sir Robert. "His response to my exclamation was, that he was fully alive to the dangers of Scheele's green—that he had written on the subject—that he had ordered a paper specially free from arsenic—that this paper, though green, was perfectly innocent,—that, in fact, there was no ground for alarm."

"But you thought otherwise?" said Mr. Fortescue.

"I was satisfied as to the danger he was incurring," replied Sir Robert; "but I could only say, 'Try it, and you will rue it; mark my words.' Mrs. Millrod thought my warning highly ridiculous, and added, *she* could speak from experience, having had a similar paper in her own boudoir for the last ten years. Her tone would have carried some weight, had not her husband, as if suddenly inspired, turned to her and said, 'Perhaps, my dear, that may account for your frequent illnesses. You know you never can remain here for a month together.'"

"A damper!" remarked Lord Henry. "Did you hear more of the hall paper?"

"I saw nothing more of the Doctor for a whole week," said Sir Robert, "at the end of which time I came across him, and saw a most woe-begone countenance. On asking the cause, his reply was, 'Oh, I have been so ill; we have all been so ill! I have had to send off Mrs. Millrod, and one of my patients has left, and I have had to remove all the rest to another part of the house. Your words have come true. It is all that horrible paper, and I have been obliged to have it down!'"

"Poor doctor! Well, at least, he was eventually open to conviction," said Lord Henry. "But what of the warranty given or implied by the paper-manufacturer that it was free from arsenic?"

"I can answer that by quoting another authority," said Mr. Herbert. "I lately met, in Devonshire, a medical man fully acquainted with the subject. He told me, when papering his house, he had been anxious to have a green paper, provided it could be a vegetable green, or anything perfectly innocuous. He had consulted his paper-hanger, who assured him his wishes could be met. The paper was accordingly selected, and the quantity required was sent to his house, each piece having the words 'Warranted free from arsenic' printed upon it. The happy idea occurred of testing it, when, to his consternation, every test gave undoubted evidence of the presence of arsenic. He added his belief that no green paper is ever made without this virulent poison."

"That very statement has been made to me by some of the first paper-manufacturers on several occasions," remarked Sir Robert, "proving that human nature is at work in that direction likewise, and establishing my proposition that we have need to look sharp for ourselves, if we value health or strength."

"I, for one, am obliged to be perpetually on the watch, after having been brought by this deceptive paper to the verge of the grave," rejoined Mr. Herbert. "Even now, when I flatter myself I have nearly got rid of its effects, I find old symptoms returning if I sit an hour in a room which has green in any part of the paper. Not long since I met a medical friend, to whom rumour had carried a report of my death, during my severe illness. He was glad to see me again on *terra firma*, and asked for particulars of my late illness. I detailed the symptoms without assigning the cause. To my surprise he asked, 'Had you green paper in your room?'"

"Had that question never occurred to your medical advisers?" asked Lord Henry.

"Never had I been questioned on the subject," said Mr. Herbert; "and I asked Dr. Lapford's reason for the inquiry. 'Some years since,' he replied, 'I was house-surgeon at one of the London hospitals. During a temporary absence on leave, my rooms were repapered, and all looked right on my return. Up to that time I had always felt fully equal to my duties, in which I took peculiar pleasure. After my return, in perfect health, all seemed gradually changed: I was unable to study as usual in the evening; drowsiness and lassitude stole over me, I felt tired and not up to my work, and was getting low and nervous, when a thought of green paper flashed across me. I tore off a piece of the paper, submitted it to chemical analyzation, discovered arsenic, had it down forthwith, and soon became as strong to labour as before.'"

"Bravo!" exclaimed Mr. Fortescue. "Herbert, you rival Chichester in your illustrative stories. Do tell us of any other doctor who has been similarly enlightened, for I never yet met with one."

"Well, the case of the late Mr. Wakley, M.P., will perhaps do as well as any. As responsible editor and proprietor of the *Lancet*, he had a room in the Strand, which happened to be hung with green paper, where he spent some hours daily. He suffered long from the usual symptoms in the eyes, nostrils, and air-passages, with general languor. The removal of the paper at length suggested itself to him as an experiment. He tried it, and these unpleasant symptoms quickly vanished. I had this on undoubted authority from a physician connected with the *Lancet*."

"Then green papers must evidently be cashiered," said Lord Henry. "But now let us place Mrs. Fortescue's inquiry before Mr. Herbert, and ask his opinion. Do you really think a slight admission of green in the paper can be seriously prejudicial where the grounding is entirely innocent of arsenic?"

"Of course, as a rule, it cannot be equally

injurious," replied Mr. Herbert; "but I have seen numerous instances of persons so susceptible to this poison that a very small proportion of arsenic is fatal to their health. Curious to say, I have just had a letter this morning which rather establishes this view of the case. The writer is a gentleman whom I happened to meet when last in the South of England. It seems that his wife's long-continued illness recalled to his mind what he had heard of my history, and he wrote to me just as I was leaving home, to inquire, with many apologies, if I thought her bedroom paper (a piece of which he enclosed) could possibly occasion her sufferings."

"The fatal green, of course," remarked Mr. Fortescue.

"Not strictly a green paper," answered Mr. Herbert. "The ground was a shade of stone, and the flowers on it partly self-coloured, picked out with green grass. But the mischief lay in a pretty ribbon of green which wreathed the whole pattern. My advice, on reading his description of her symptoms was to remove it, and it appears he has done so. I will read the sequel in his own words: 'The day after I wrote to you our medical man called in, and I mentioned to him my fears regarding the papering. He immediately said he had a patient suffering in precisely the same way from a green papering, and that he had no doubt of its being the cause of my wife's illness. I lost no time therefore in having it removed. My wife feels already sensibly better, but intends, if she feels any further ill-effects, adopting your kind advice as to the baths. At my father's, Ardley Court, I quite think one of my sisters is suffering from the same cause, and the paper, containing plenty of arsenical poisoning, is also condemned. A friend of ours was mentioning yesterday that he could give twenty cases in which people had, to his own knowledge, been affected by this poisonous paper.' The writer goes on, naturally enough, to enlarge upon the impropriety of such papers being permitted to be made and sold in England.

"He must be thankful, however, that he met in you one able and willing to warn him," said Mr. Fortescue; "for though his doctor gave a sensible assent, when questioned as to the danger, it would seem that he had not previously suggested it as the cause of the lady's illness. We owe you many thanks, Herbert, for your additions to our rapidly-increasing store of facts relating to the green paper subject. I am quite unconscious of ever having been poisoned myself, still I have made up my mind not to run the risk any longer of poisoning my friends. Therefore, upon any 'verdant assassins,' as Chichester calls them, which may be in my house I have resolved to execute summary justice as soon as I return home. I will not *hang*, but simply banish, every one of them."

"And I," said Lord Henry, "will promise to adopt a similar course when I have a house of my own. Meanwhile, what of our projected excursion on the Lake? Can we tempt Mr. Herbert to accompany us?"

"I have an engagement, unfortunately, in another direction," returned Mr. Herbert; "but I trust we may meet again *en face* Mont Blanc. I hear you are off towards Chamounix to-morrow, and I hope to find you there, unless you linger *en route*. If so, 'perchance our meeting next may fall' at Thun, in the Vaudois Highlands, or at Martigny. *Au revoir.*"

CHAPTER XIV.

INSURMOUNTABLE PREJUDICES.

"Yet what petition could avail,
    Or who would listen to the tale?"—*Marmion.*
"Why sleeps he not when others are at rest?"—BYRON.

Vallées des Ormonts.

"WELCOME, Herbert!" said Mr. Fortescue, who was the first to espy his friend as he walked into the Hotel of the Aigle d'Or at Sepay. "You have indeed overtaken us as you threatened. Now give an account of yourself and your route."

"Curious to say, I have followed so completely in your track, that you may yourself write the latter," returned Mr. Herbert. "At Thun, at Erlenbach, in the Simmenthal, and onwards, everywhere I saw inscribed the names of Lord H. Douglass, Sir R. Chichester, and that of my honourable friend in the hotel books."

"Indeed! Did you then chance to fall in with a certain Admiral Courtland?" inquired Lord Henry.

"There was an old naval officer, apparently in ill health, at Château d'Œx, and I think I remember seeing the name, but I did not make his acquaintance," replied Mr. Herbert.

"That was a pity," rejoined Lord Henry; "for Sir Robert tried to convince him that he was a victim to arsenical poisoning, and you of course would have hit the nail on the head."

"Was he convinced in part?" asked Mr. Herbert.

"Well, he seemed inclined to allow that some of his walls were covered with green paper," replied Lord Henry; "but he thought Chichester must be falsely accusing them, inasmuch as he had had the first London advice, and no hint had ever been given him to that effect."

"Alas!" returned Mr. Herbert, "too often patients may be in their graves if they must wait for an intimation of danger from such a quarter. Just before leaving town, I had occasion to see one of the most enlightened of the Faculty at his own house. In passing an open door I saw some of the green of the period, to which I called his attention. You do not think there is any harm in that?' was his smiling remark. Well, in the presence of so great a man, what could I do but humbly hint at an unquestionable fact, when he stopped me by saying, 'Oh, yes, but what you allude to is green *flock* paper; there certainly is sometimes danger in *that*."

"What would our poor friend Mrs. Mackenzie have said to this, Chichester?" inquired Mr. Fortescue.

"What, indeed! and the hosts of other victims to the drawing-room and bed-room papers which both Mr. Herbert and myself have known. But, as regards flock paper, I remember Dr. Lapford assuring me that, if any green papers must be tolerated, the flock was decidedly the least dangerous.* And he gave a very satisfactory explanation of his views by pointing out that the wool on the flock paper, itself innocent, catches and retains much of the arsenical dust which would otherwise be floating about the room."

"Sensible man!" said Mr. Herbert. "I feel peculiarly thankful when I find medical testimony yielding an assent to recent discoveries, whether of malefic influences heretofore unsuspected, or of agencies for coping with such evils hitherto untried. My sphere of observation of medical men, and of the almost unbounded influence exerted by them over their patients,

*See Note C in the Appendix.

has been unusually large. And recognizing as I do the laborious, self-denying, unwearied attention to the duties of their profession, the large-heartedness and high-mindedness which characterize a very large number of the disciples of Esculapius, I yet must say that there is amongst them as great an amount of prejudice as amongst any body of men I have met. There exists, in fact, at this present day as proverbial an antipathy to the discoveries of science as there was in the days of the immortal Harvey, when scarcely one of his brethren who had attained the age of forty would admit the theory of the circulation of the blood."

"I am afraid my observation is but confirmatory of your own," said Sir Robert. "I find the doctors usually my most formidable opponents when I strive to convince my friends that prejudicial results can possibly ensue from daily inhaling poison."

"But how do you account for it," said Lord Henry, "that our English medicos have been hitherto so slow either to detect the danger which has, perhaps in consequence, now grown into such wide-spread proportions, or to admit the virtue of the remedies which you have proved so powerful?"

"Partly, perhaps, from considering it needful to

know only such dangers as orthodoxy has laid down on the medical map, but still more from an intense desire to avoid any recognition of new discoveries which they view as quackery," replied Sir Robert; "and so, in their efforts to steer clear of Scylla, they engulf their poor patients in Charybdis. Some day they will ignore their own prejudices, which are now unconsciously giving way before the light cast on their pathway by their yet unrequited fellow-labourers in the field of medical science."

"But the non-medical public need surely not be so straitlaced," said Lord Henry.

"One would think not," replied Sir Robert; "but it would be as easy to persuade a Chinese to abandon his opium, as to induce one's friends to give up inhaling their arsenic against their own wills while it is sanctioned by their medical men. Here is a recent instance: Lady Chichester has been spending a month with our friends the Howards. Lady Elizabeth has been in a very sad state of health for the last two years—you remember her, Fortescue?—and I will just read you part of Lady Chichester's letter respecting her. She says: 'I do so regret my inability to sound an effectual note of warning here, as to the danger of arsenic in the wall-papers.

Dear Lady Elizabeth is still a sad sufferer, and the strange part is, though she has had the very first advice, that no one can satisfactorily explain or account for her illness. The only hope from the first held out has been that it will " wear itself out." My own dread is lest it may wear her out first. After watching your mysterious illness so closely, and knowing its origin, you will understand my anxiety when I tell you she has a plentiful sprinkling of arsenic in her bedroom paper. I believe I may truly say poor Lady E. has not had a good night's rest for now two years. From eight or ten thousand leaves of arsenical green in her paper, many thousand grains of this poison must be constantly discharging their dust; and as she often spends fourteen hours out of the twenty-four in her bedroom, can we wonder at their injurious effect on her nervous system? However, as Dr. Vaughan, the great medical authority of the West of England, is in constant attendance, it is useless to say more than I have already ventured to do.' "

" There appears to be a kind of glamour which hovers over the medical vision as regards this especial danger," said Mr. Herbert; "still I believe with you, Sir Robert, that the day will come when they will be only too anxious to ignore the fact that they ever disregarded it."

"This is a melancholy case," said Mr. Fortescue. "Do you suppose that green paper originated Lady Elizabeth's illness? and is there no hope of her changing it if only as an experiment?"

"It is impossible, apparently, to say what originated her illness," answered Sir Robert; "but it is evident that, under the nervous irritation induced by chronic suffering, recovery is likely to be greatly retarded, to say the least of it, by the continual presence of a poisonous agent, which she is perpetually inhaling, and with the noxious properties of which you are now well acquainted. Lady Chichester goes on to say: 'I think I might succeed with Lady E., but Mr. Howard, kind as he is, is resolute in his endeavours to think it all a myth. I could wish, for his own sake, he would banish every atom of this slow poison, for he, too, has not been the thing."

"One would think," said Lord Henry, "that two years of suffering were sufficient to make one willing to try any remedy suggested."

"If it emanated from a medical man it would be thought orthodox, and instantly followed," replied Sir Robert; "but coming, as in this case, from those who can speak from practical experience only, it is regarded as quackery, and shares the usual fate of 'advice gratis.' Howard, however, goes to the extent of admitting that it may be unadvisable to have a paper wholly green."

"Yet, if no poison exists in the leaves, or in a partial grounding," said Lord Henry, "by a parity of reasoning, none can be found in the larger quantity. Perhaps, however, when these obnoxious papers have been up any length of time, the danger diminishes."

"Not in the slightest degree," returned Sir Robert. "Remember the illustration of the musk, which retains its properties unimpaired for half a century, or more. If arsenic were similarly scented, you would be as conscious of its presence when your green paper had been hung fifty years as when first put up."

"But is there no simple test by which the presence of arsenic in the paper can be approximately ascertained?" asked Lord Henry.

"There are several," replied Mr. Herbert. "I always use one recommended by Professor Hoffmann as the simplest, and he says, in nine cases out of ten, sufficient. Apply a drop of strong spirits of ammonia to the suspected green and it will turn it blue, and when dry leave a yellow spot. Only be careful to keep your spirits well stoppered—not corked, or the effects will evaporate."

"I will always carry a bottle with me," said Lord Henry. "But would not your test turn *any* green blue?"

"No; it will usually have no more effect than a drop of water, when arsenite of copper is not present," answered Mr. Herbert. "There are *very few* other than arsenical greens that would be at all affected by this test."

"You spoke of electricity as a curative agent, Herbert," said Mr. Fortescue; "do give us some scientific explanation of the same. We ought to go home primed not only as to the danger, but also as to a remedy."

"Willingly," said Mr. Herbert; "but having come this morning from Rossinières, although I have only actually walked from La Comballa, I must plead guilty to fatigue; and as we shall probably take some excursion this afternoon, I must indulge in repose till dinner-time."

"Indeed you ought to do so," said his friend. "And now to draw your attention for one moment to the scenery around. What think you of this green sward stretching far down into the valley of the Rhone? of that glorious panorama of snowy mountains—the range of the Trient—some sixty miles distant? and this purest of atmospheres, sufficient to counteract all the arsenic you may have imbibed?"

"Pure indeed," said Mr. Herbert. "In the Vaudois highlands one seems able to appreciate the infinite goodness which has made mere existence a source of exquisite enjoyment. Look at the sunlit little church embowered in those dark pine firs, and those picturesque Swiss cottages constituting Les Ormonts, dotted everywhere around and down the valley. They say the fear of fire suggested the idea of each châlet being far apart from its wooden neighbour; but, be that as it may, all artists must rejoice at the result. I must really establish myself in yonder window facing the Dent du Midi, and abandon myself to a contemplation of the scene."

CHAPTER XV.

AN ELECTRIC CURE.

"When energizing objects men pursue,
What is the miracle they cannot do?"

Glaciers des Diablerets.

IN the afternoon Mr. Herbert had sufficiently recovered his fatigues of the morning to join the tourists in an excursion to the stern-looking glaciers of the Diablerets. The smiling beauty of the *Plan des Isles*, confronting these icy barriers, tempted them to linger, and sketch, and admire, till the descending sun urged their homeward route.

"And now, Percy," said Mr. Fortescue, in returning, "having just come from one of Nature's grandest efforts, let us return to her laws, which you promised this morning to unfold to us. Having aided Chichester in scaring us from using the green of the period, the least you can do, by way of *amende honorable*, is to give us a remedy to hand over to any sufferers from the same we may chance to encounter."

"You allude, I presume, to the electro-chemical baths which I found so beneficial in extracting the said poison, and restoring life and health?" returned his friend. "Suppose, then, I commence with certain propositions as well known to you as to myself. *Imprimis*: Electricity is one of the chief essential elements of life. It is, in fact, the very essence of animal life. Take away electricity, and you take away life. Restore the due balance of electricity in the system, and you restore the vital power and functions. Electricity penetrates and permeates the whole human frame. Without electricity the blood would not circulate. Nerve and muscle are alike subject to its influence. The very air we breathe is charged with electricity, and the food we eat by decomposition evolves electricity."

"Yes, those are undeniable axioms," said Mr. Fortescue, "but how do you proceed to apply them?"

"Simply thus. Electricity has long been recognized as a remedial agent in cases of dyspepsia, and in paralytic and other affections. It eliminates from the tissues, membranes, and even the very pores of the body all inert and inorganic substances which are foreign, and therefore noxious, to the system. We all agree that to be stout is no sign of health, and the explanation is this: Food taken into the system, if it does not nourish, poisons the blood. The atmosphere we inhale, when foul or vitiated, acts in a similar manner.

"Hence, therefore, the mischief you attribute to your green paper?" said Mr. Fortescue.

"You are right. I was going on to speak of a safety-valve, if we only understood it aright. Nature rejects this poison in a thousand ways. Sometimes she testifies her displeasure by stirring up irritation and rebellion in the central states; sometimes by exciting to inflammation or fever-heat; at other times she exerts her strength to expel the offender bodily to the uttermost region of her territories, in the form of eruptions, or in accumulating and massing together inert fleshy substances which we call undue fatness, and which produce heaviness and discomfort to the whole system. Now electricity attacks this enemy in all its secret ramifications—goes at once to the root of the evil, follows it through all its hidden recesses, and is a match for it in mines and counter-mines. It detects and drives out the enemy wheresoever he may lurk, in the tissues, fibres, nerves, muscles, morbific formations, bones, and brain all alike, and will give 'no quarter.'"

"One would think, Mr. Herbert, you were an army doctor," exclaimed Lord Henry. "It is rather awful to regard one's self as the seat of war! You almost carry me back in imagination to the Crimea, and remind me of some slashing work we had there in dislodging the foe.

"Well, it is just that," returned Mr. Herbert, "As long as the enemy is suffered to entrench himself behind his strong fortress, your most brilliant feat of arms in the open field will do him but little damage."

"I see it clearly," rejoined Sir Robert. "Disease is the landing of the enemy and his entrenchment behind his earthworks. Electricity is your battery by which you force him to beat a retreat."

"Precisely so," answered Mr. Herbert. "Disease is a foreign element in the body. Nature is ever striving to regain its normal state of health and happiness. Electricity, and especially that mode of applying it which is adopted in the electro-chemical bath, lends Nature the most efficient aid towards accomplishing her purpose."

"I am glad you have arrived at that point," said

Lord Henry Douglass; "for I had previously understood you to say your own cure was effected by means of some baths; and interesting as this little disquisition on electricity has been, I could not quite see its connexion with baths. How is it? Do you receive a shock under water? or is the bath the conductor of the electricity?"

"The inventor of the baths to which I alluded," answered Mr. Herbert, "is a French M.D., who has devoted his life to the study of electricity as a curative agent. He is a member of many learned societies in France, England, and America; and I have reason to be thankful when I add that he has taken up his abode in London. Before leaving home I put one of his little pamphlets in my portmanteau, and this afternoon, as Fortescue wished for information on the subject, I brought it out with me."

"Capital!" said Mr. Fortescue. "You will now be able to let your French M.D. speak for himself. What is his name?"

"His name is Dr. Caplin, and his massive forehead and benevolent countenance, corresponding with his avowed aim in all his discoveries of benefiting suffering humanity, inspires you with confidence in his system. His motto is—

"'What art cannot perform,
Nature accomplishes.'

But to quote from his pamphlet:—

"'THE ELECTRO-CHEMICAL BATH is a bath by means of which *electricity* is so applied as to promote all the *chemical* phenomena of the human organism.

"'This mode of applying electricity differs from all other methods hitherto employed, as being a means by which the electric fluid is introduced at once and directly *into the whole body*, and thereby acts upon all the vital organs, instead of being applied locally, or externally, upon the mere periphery of the body, as practised in all other systems.

"'The distinctive *modus operandi* of the bath is that, instead of producing a *single* current, it forms as many currents as there are pores on the skin;— *i.e.*, seven or eight millions, according to the stature or bulk of the patient.

"'It is now more than thirteen years since this discovery was made by Dr. Caplin; and, as the merits of the bath have been fully tested during that period, he has no hesitation in speaking of its efficacy in almost every disease, and in recommending it with confidence to sufferers as NATURE'S UNIVERSAL PANACEA.

"'The truth of this annunciation is proved by the fact that many diseases, abandoned as hopeless and incurable, both in private and hospital practice, have been radically cured by means of the *Electro-Chemical Bath*, in conjunction with local application of electricity.'"

"And you endorse all this from your own experience, Herbert?" inquired Mr. Fortescue.

"My experience extends merely to my own case, and that of a few others whom I have induced to follow my example," replied Mr. Herbert. "When one has, however, received sensible and great benefit one's self from any novel mode of treatment, I always feel it as a duty to mankind at large, and to one's friends in particular, to make them acquainted with it."

"But the theory commends itself to your judgment," suggested Mr. Fortescue.

"Indeed it does so," replied his friend, "as being simple, rational, and effective. In examining new claims to scientific and medical discoveries, I always proceed upon three assumptions: first, that no existing human system can be perfect; the second, that at least a fragment of truth underlies almost every system; and thirdly, that we are as yet but upon the threshold of medical science; and however original and profound my first proposition may be considered, in my third I am happy to know I am borne out by the concurrent testimony of some of our ablest medical men. My second aspect of the case induces me to investigate new discoveries, especially those intended to ameliorate human suffering, and not to discard them untried merely because they are new.

"It is somewhat strange, Herbert, that one has never heard of these said baths," remarked Mr. Fortescue. "You spoke of having tried them, Chichester, but never before have I met with an allusion to them. Where are they to be found? and are they generally known?"

"They ought to be more extensively known by this time than they are," replied Sir Robert, "having now been established in London, at 9, York Place, Portman Square, for about thirteen years. I can never be sufficiently thankful that I was induced to try them, and only regret that I had not known them earlier."

"Well, although in neither your experience nor in Herbert's did your medico prove equal to the emergency so far as to discover the cause of your illness," said Mr. Fortescue, "I hope they were at least prompt to acknowledge the fact of the cure, and the efficacy of the means by which it had been effected?"

"As regards the latter, that would be too much to expect," replied Sir Robert, "as those means were novel to them, and of recent discovery. Whatever mischief red-tapeism may have produced at the Horse Guards, its action in that quarter is a joke when compared with the force with which it operates in the medical profession. Why, a doctor would be black-balled who ventured to subscribe to a doctrine not yet endorsed by the enlightened College of Physicians. Is not that your opinion, Mr. Herbert?"

"I fear I must reply in the affirmative," answered Mr. Herbert, smiling. "I remember once speaking to a London physician of deservedly high standing, since gone to his rest, of some of the then recent discoveries in medical lore to which I owed a debt of gratitude. In a burst of thankfulness that my lot had been cast in this latter half of the nineteenth century, when science is daily lending its aid to remedial discoveries, I unwisely mentioned that during a dangerous illness I had owed my life to hydropathy and homœopathy. Instead of the sympathy I expected, he gave me a solemn warning against the very remedies which had saved me. 'Can you, Mr. Herbert,' he exclaimed, 'wonder at the errors and heresies in religion, which are springing up on all sides, while you lend the weight of your influence to that which you must know to be equal heresy in medecine?'

"I ventured to plead personal experience and observation, and to reason upon well-known laws of nature. In vain. The great College of doctors had pronounced against some of my newly-adopted remedies, and ignored others, and evidently I ought to have preferred an orthodox death under mistaken medical treatment to a life purchased upon such heretical terms. Naturally we differed; and here I am alive and well to show the effects of being open to conviction, and of resorting on more occasions than one to unorthodox, common-sense remedies.

"But, Herbert," said Mr. Fortescue, "I think so clever a man as you say Dr. Caplin is, ought to take some means of making his medical brethren acquainted with his discoveries."

"He has taken every pains so to do," replied Mr. Herbert. "If you like to look at this pamphlet, you see will he challenges the profession at large to come and examine his system and judge for themselves. He says he has repeatedly published this challenge in different medical journals, but hitherto, apparently, pretty much in vain."

"Well, evidently the doctor has done all in his power to communicate the knowledge of this valuable discovery," said Mr. Fortescue, returning the book. "Have you any notion how it has been taken? You have both doubtless spoken to your own medical men respecting it."

"I will first answer for myself," said Sir Robert. "Lady Chichester, as soon as she saw the beneficial effects of Dr. Caplin's system upon me, and understood somewhat of the theory, went off to Dr. Farrier, desirous of having her own hopes confirmed by his high sanction. To her surprise she encountered nothing but ridicule: 'Is it possible, Lady Chichester, that a woman of your sense can credit such a fable as the extraction of the substances of which you speak?' In some consternation she inquired if he had really detected any imposture—whether he spoke from his own knowledge after having examined and tested the operation of the baths? Not he, indeed! He had too much sense and too little time to run after such absurdities."

"Safe ground certainly on which to condemn a new invention," said Lord Henry. "If I were ill, I think I should prefer a medico who ventured to save life by adopting even the most recent panacea which had proved itself effectual in other cases. I think the great thing is to be prepared to grasp truth as we find it, and to be ready to investigate new discoveries. Without this we might still be roasting inside red curtains for scarlet fever, as the only cure known to our forefathers."

"And condemning the Galileos of our own day to the Inquisition for asserting and maintaining that the earth goes round," added Mr. Herbert.

"'*E pur se muove,*'" said Lord Henry. "And here we are once more looking down on little Sepay. We leave this to-morrow for Martigny, Mr. Herbert, first to visit the monks of St. Bernard, and the next day we are off to Chamounix. You will now, I hope, accompany us?"

"As far as St. Maurice, I shall be most happy to go with you," replied Mr. Herbert; "but from thence I have promised to pay a visit to a friend who is staying at the Baths of Lavey. I hope, however, to rejoin you at Martigny, in time to scale the Forclaz and cross the Tête Noir with you."

CHAPTER XVI.

AUTHORITATIVE TESTIMONY.

"Alas! for the writer who dares undertake
To urge reformation of national ill;
His head and his heart are both likely to ache
With the double employment of logic and quill."
—*Cowper*.

"'Tis but a single murder."—*Fatal Curiosity*.

Chamounix.

"CHICHESTER, with whom were you in such close confab just now?" inquired Mr. Fortescue. "I thought at first it was the doctor with whom we crossed the Channel."

"No, not himself, but one of the fraternity," replied Sir Robert; "and the likeness was rather striking. I was having some interesting conversation with him, and found him a most intelligent and well-informed man."

"On the subject of green paper, eh?"

"I am afraid you take me for a monomaniac, Fortescue. We actually conversed for half an hour without touching on green paper. We were comparing the glaciers here with those of Iceland, which appear to present the same phenomena of progression and retrogression; and from them we naturally glided off to the Geysers, which he had visited and I had not; and then we discussed the theory of the gulf stream, and congratulated ourselves that, while possessing in England a Siberian latitude, we owed to its influence so mild a climate. Thankful, too, that the Mer de Glace, so beautiful to the eyes of summer tourists, was not transferred to the Vale of Taunton, for instance."

"But at the end of the half-hour?"

"Well, I am free to confess that the subject was finally broached," answered Sir Robert. "But when I tell you I discovered my friend to be Dr. Merton, of Harley Street, Cavendish Square, who was himself one of the earliest victims to this dangerous paper, you will scarcely wonder that we, as fellow-sufferers, compared notes."

"He also has really had personal experience of its baneful effects?" asked Lord Henry.

"Yes, he gave me an account of it. His illness

was marked by the usual symptoms, and so ill was he that several of his professional brethren were consulted on his case. They sent him abroad in quest of cure; and though he returned well, yet, as soon as he resumed practice, his old symptoms reappeared. It was unanimously agreed that he must again leave home, and temporarily, if not entirely, give up his practice, when the green paper of his study happily occurred to him. It was tested, condemned, and taken down, and his own resuscitation, and resumption of health and practice followed."

"Capital!" said Lord Henry; "I suppose he swelled your budget of anecdotes. Do give us some, Chichester."

"He mentioned a case of insanity," replied Sir Robert, "which had arisen entirely from the same cause, and about which he had lately been consulted; and more than one instance of paralysis having been produced by this dreaded agency, and which he had detected."

"It would really be in the interest of suffering humanity for a few more doctors to be poisoned," said Lord Henry. "It would put them on the *qui vive* as regards their patients."

"Then you will rejoice to hear the case of a medical

friend of Dr. Merton's, who, like himself, was poisoned by green paper in his study," rejoined Sir Robert. "After discovering the cause of his malady, he resorted to Turkish baths and obtained a cure; and, in a fit of enthusiastic gratitude, he got up a company and has opened a 'Hammam' at Brighton. Dr. Merton also lent me an old number of the *London Review*, containing a paper written by Dr. Orton, whose name you may remember in connexion with the Limehouse case. I will, if you like, read you parts of it."

"By all means," said both his friends.

In detailing the first case which came under his notice, and which led eventually to his investigations and conclusions concerning this fatal green of the period, Dr. Orton writes: 'I was baffled at every step I took in the curative process. The symptoms changing about, never continuing two days alike, it was my lot to see her one day with low fever, on another cheerful, enjoying her food, with a promise of speedy recovery. Then, in the midst of this state of things, I was sent for suddenly. The child was dying! And this was the progress during the thirteen days—now better, now worse, now dying. Four times had I been sent for in this time to tell me the child was dying. On these occasions, from some unnoticeable and inappreciable cause, she had fallen into a brief state of syncope. On the last summons, as usual, the child rallied a little; but the small thready pulse told its tale too well, and in an hour she died.'

"It makes me shudder," said Sir Robert Chichester, as he paused in reading, "to think how similar was my own case; and had I not, as I told you, been led by accident to abandon my verdant quarter almost at the last moment, I should not, I verily believe, be here now."

"But as you are, my dear fellow, do read us some more from the *Review*," said Lord Henry. "I want to go home thoroughly up in the subject."

"Well, then, here is another case. Dr. Orton says: 'On the 26th of May, just one month afterwards, a Mrs. Owen called to consult me. She said she had been for ten weeks complaining of headache, pain over the brows, smarting of the eyes, defective sight, irritation of the nostrils and upper lip, tenderness of the mouth and gums, all the teeth aching, throat dry, with pain at the epigastrium, at times very severe, short, dry, hacking cough, breathing short, general tremor, great prostration, loss of appetite. She had not rested well for weeks, and the symptoms were always worse in the morning, particularly in the running of the eyes and headache. In a moment I suspected arsenical poisoning! This cluster of symptoms belonged to no disease with which I was acquainted. One question was enough; the house had been papered with green paper about ten weeks, just so long as she had been a sufferer.'

"'Again, her father and mother slept in a room covered with green paper; and the father, who rose early for his morning's work, suffered a little, but the mother, who remained, endured much more.

"'But yet again; her three sisters slept in a room where there was no green paper, and they were quite well.'

"Details follow," said Sir Robert, "which I need not read, as to the opinion given, and happily attended to. The paper continues:—

"'In two days I saw her again, in company with her husband. The paper had been removed; but it had made him sick and ill whilst doing it. She was much better, was able to eat, and felt stronger in every way. The children, too, for the first time for weeks, had been playing and running about all day long. She further said, as respected herself, that for the last few weeks she had become almost blind, and, though only twenty-eight, was unable to see without glasses.* But now; in the short space of four days, her sight was beginning to return. I considered this case so extraordinary, so perfect a type of arsenical poisoning, that I besought the attendance of two respectable tradesmen to be present with Mrs. Owen and her husband, and to question them. The result was that a document was drawn up noting the facts, signed by the principals, and unhesitatingly attested.'

"Dr. Orton goes on to adduce other cases, but all with marked similarity of type. I will therefore just read the winding-up of the paper.

"'Finally, my conclusions on the whole question of arsenical poisoning from the use of wall paper, deduced from a very close and watchful experience, are contained in the following propositions:—

"'1. That arsenical paper in house decoration is dangerous from two modes in which the poison may be conveyed to the system: in the form of particles of the arsenical salt floating in the atmosphere, and

---

* A paper by Dr. Alfred Taylor will be found in the Appendix, reprinted from the Reports of the Ophthalmic Hospital, proving that ophthalmia is a result of using arsenical paper-hangings.

possibly in the more subtle, but not the less certain, mode of arsenuretted hydrogen gas.

"'2. That the arsenical particles or dust, from attrition or concussion of the walls, are more readily to be apprehended in dry weather and in heated rooms; although during summer, from a freer ventilation, by the door and windows being open, the poison is then *comparatively* innocuous.

"'3. That the heavy damp weather is the season of most peril, and that *then, by a decomposition set on foot, the poison is insidiously conveyed to the system* in the form of arsenuretted hydrogen gas.

"'4. That this poison affects *persons of all ages* coming under its influence, but that it is more remarkably obnoxious to infantile life.

"'5. That arsenic so absorbed is not uniform in its action, varying from slight, little noticeable, up to serious symptoms, being modified by idiosyncrasy and other circumstances; but *that the mucous membrane is peculiarly the seat of its attack*, as manifested in its simulation of the various forms of diphtheria, in producing ophthalmia, defective vision, nasal irritation, partial salivation, burning sensation in the throat, great thirst, short dry cough, even asthma, low fever, great prostration, and faintings.

"'6. That the most susceptible time of its action on children is, it is believed, after the occurrence of eruptive fevers, as measles, scarlatina, &c., just when the vital powers are at the lowest state, and when the absorbents are resuming vigorous action; and then, under the predicated conditions, diarrhœa, and other analogous disorders, frequently lead to serious results.

"'7. That it is considered probable, if not certain, that much baffling disease, already characterized, is often found in medical practice not amenable to ordinary remedies, but which will readily succumb (as has been experienced in numerous instances) on a removal of the patient from the sphere of this poisonous influence.'"

"Thanks, Chichester. That paper is most conclusive," said Lord Henry. "But how, in the face of all this evidence circulating through the country, can these papers be tolerated? I suppose the fashion must at the least be on the wane?"

"Well, is it so?" said Mr. Fortescue. "In the last letter I received from Mrs. Fortescue, she tells me that she agreed to spend a week at Oxford in company with the friends she had been visiting. Rooms were bespoken for them at an hotel, all of which were thus decorated. On remarking it to the chambermaid, she said it was the case nearly all through the house."

"And I," said Mr. Herbert, who had joined their party, "lately went to call on some friends of mine who had come up to an hotel in Piccadilly. I found the sitting-room papered with a green flock, the same paper in one bed-room, and a pale green in the other, so there was not a room in which I could remain with safety."

"Thus this is a mischief which is pervading all classes," said Sir Robert, "rich and poor alike. Well, indeed, may we exclaim with a writer in the daily press, when speaking of this and other forms of poison introduced by recent fashion, 'How many of the diseases which fill our hospitals, how many of the miserable stunted growths and helpless feeble frames which hang idly about our streets, are the results of all these slow poisonings, kept up from infancy to age with relentless cruelty, it is impossible to calculate.'"

"Then the green of the period must take rank as a British grievance, which they say has as many lives as a cat," remarked Lord Henry. "One would think it could never survive a day if all the facts you have told us were made publicly known; but Englishmen are proverbially long-suffering on such points. So let us now go out and compose ourselves under the shadow of Mont Blanc.

CHAPTER XVII.

DEATH ON THE WALLS.

"Is it lawful to save life—or to kill?"

Mont Blanc.

"TALKING of hotels," said Sir Robert Chichester, in answer to an observation of Lord Henry Douglass, as they were returning from the source of the Arveiron, on the following day, "I must not forget to tell you one of Dr. Merton's adventures which he mentioned to me yesterday.

"It was his intention to take down his family to enjoy the beauties of the North Devon coast this summer during his absence from England. A friend was staying at a large and very comfortable Hotel at Harm-with-combe, facing the sea, and thither he bent his steps. On being shown his bedroom, he found the verdant assassin lying in wait, and asked for another apartment. Room after room was offered him, but in every one the mischief, either fullblown or in the bud, was at work, and he was upon the point of quitting the hotel in disgust, when they managed to find a room in which he could repose in peace. But, alas! only for one night, for on entering the dining-room, to his dismay, he found a green flock paper, and he had to go elsewhere for a dinner. The public coffee-room was also green; and this at a spot the most salubrious in North Devon, where people resort for health!"

"Of course he drew his friend's attention to it," remarked Mr. Fortescue.

"He did so," answered Sir Robert. "The reply was, 'It is true it pervades the house, but I never thought of it till you mentioned it. Can it possibly account for the fact that almost every one here complains of something the matter with their throats? I have been here for a month. We sometimes sit down 150 at the table d'hôte, and I have been quite struck with the frequency of throat complaints. Also, curious to say, I have almost lost my appetite since I came here; but as the air has so high a repute for salubrity, I could not account for it.'"

"But Dr. Merton could," said Lord Henry. "Well, evidently, as we agreed before, the poisonous effects of the 'Green of the Period' must then be classed amongst 'things not generally known.'"

"Aroused as your attention now is to the subject, Lord Henry," said Mr. Herbert, "you will be amazed to find that there is scarcely an hotel in England, or a house where apartments are 'to let,' where this pernicious fashion does not prevail. The exceptions are so rare that they prove the rule."

"I wish, Chichester," said Mr. Fortescue, "that all who have been similarly victimized were as energetic in warning their friends and acquaintances as you and Herbert are. The evil might then have been eradicated by this time. One must surely have come across other victims before now."

"Apart from the fatal indifference which in such matters characterizes most people, you may not have encountered those who have purchased their knowledge as dearly as we have done," returned Sir Robert, "and that which costs us little is usually little prized."

"Lightly won, loosely worn," rejoined Lord Henry; "but Fortescue and myself must endeavour to prove exceptions to the rule."

"I suppose in your large parish, Herbert, you often trace its ill-effects," said Mr. Fortescue.

"Indeed I do, and often meditate upon the best means of overcoming public apathy and ignorance with regard to it. I have tried to induce various periodicals to write it down, but in vain. The excuse given by one editor was that 'every educated person was so well acquainted with the subject, that further information was unnecessary.' But I must own this is totally opposed to my experience in the matter."

"How did you become yourself convinced?" asked Lord Henry.

"I suffered martyrdom for years," replied Mr. Herbert, "but without knowing the cause. I think it was first suggested to me by one of my parishioners, who told me a melancholy instance of its danger. A friend of hers, with only two children, had lately taken a new house near London where the nurseries were thus adorned. Soon medical attendance was required for the previously fine healthy children. One died, and, to the inexpressible grief of the parents, the other, despite the utmost care, and calling in further advice, soon followed. While the little corpse was lying in the house, the father was told of the properties of green paper, and a *post-mortem* examination was urged. He assented, and arsenic was proved to be the cause of death. The body of the first child was then exhumed, and, to their horror, arsenic was again detected in quantities sufficient to have caused its death!"

"You must have felt such a warning almost as a voice from the grave. Did the removal of your paper effect a cure?" asked Mr. Fortescue.

"Not of itself," replied Mr. Herbert. "The almost magical power of electricity, as conveyed through Dr. Caplin's baths, was needed to restore life, so nearly had it ebbed. These baths have the two-fold effect of drawing out any latent poison in the system, and of restoring to it lost tone and vitality; no medicine can thus act."

"Fortescue pronounced us to be a pair, Mr. Herbert," said Sir Robert, "as regarded our store of facts, but certainly we are singularly circumstanced as to our sufferings and means of cure. I think, however, we have neither mentioned one symptom which was noticeable in my case."

"What was that?" inquired Mr. Herbert.

"A twelvemonth before the arsenical discovery," replied Sir Robert, "Dr. B——, of Mayfair applied his stethoscope to my heart, and thought there was serious mischief going on. He said little to me at the time; but two years after, when Turkish and other baths had drawn off much of the poisonous effects, I was persuaded by Lady Chichester to see him again. After a long and careful examination, Dr. B—— laid down his stethoscope and said, 'I never met with such a case in all my experience! When I saw you last, I do not hesitate to say your heart was in a most alarming state, and I should not have been surprised had I heard of your death. Now I could as confidently pronounce your heart to be as sound as any man's in London.'

"Upon further conversation Dr. B—— assured me that had that state of the heart proceeded from natural causes, perfect recovery would have been impossible; that proof was thus afforded that the previous had been an abnormal condition, and that it had been produced by the arsenic. He showed me some medical works containing *post-mortem* examinations after arsenical poisoning, where a similar state of the heart, and weakening of its walls had been perceptible. He added with emphasis, "Yours was *an arsenical heart.*"'"

"You have, indeed, had a narrow escape," said Mr. Herbert, "and, like myself, doubtless feel bound to communicate your dearly-bought knowledge."

"Yes, but in spite of such communications, I actually find some of the warned papering their walls with green grounds and green leaves, just as if all were a myth! Many, however, who would on no account have a green grounding, forget the mathematical axiom that the greater includes the less, and that the mischief which they allow exists in the grounding is precisely the same in its proportion when it only appears in the leaves. Take your child to visit a mild case of scarletina, and do not be surprised if the infection communicated results in a fatal case of scarlet fever."

"Well, I never saw it in that strong light before, Chichester," said Lord Henry, "but there is some truth in it."

"I can give an instance of the misconception which prevails on that subject," said Mr. Herbert. "Being invited to a friend's house in Wiltshire, I wrote, with many apologies and explanations, to ask if I should find my foe in my bedroom. The reply was, 'We are fully aware of the danger, and have no green paper in the house.' Thus reassured, I went, but on being shown to my room found an elegant paper of fuchsias reposing on a pale green grounding! Five bedrooms in succession were offered to me, and only one was altogether free from arsenic; but, as the other papers were not wholly and entirely green, my friends had no idea that any danger could lurk in their rooms, still less that some thousand green leaves could contain a thousand grains of arsenic."

"Well, one can quite understand such misconception on the part of those who have not paid such a penalty as you have done," said Mr. Fortescue.

"I can fully corroborate all you said just now Mr. Herbert, regarding hotels and houses to let," remarked Sir Robert, "for when travelling I have the greatest difficulty in avoiding my foe. I am very partial to a quiet little watering-place, which may be unknown to you—Northend—where a terrace has recently been built on the cliff. The situation is most inviting, and would often tempt me to make it a temporary residence. But, alas! I am compelled to avoid it, for there is not a single house in that terrace where one or more of the sitting-rooms is not hung with bright green paper.

"I lately paid a visit," added Sir Robert, "to some friends in Somersetshire. The lady of the house was mourning the loss of a much-valued housekeeper, who had accompanied them thither in perfect health, but had been taken mysteriously ill, and had been obliged to leave. My own history having often formed the topic of conversation, my friend asked one day if green paper could possibly have caused her servant's unaccountable illness. Of course I was unable to say, until she suggested that they should show me the bedroom which the housekeeper had occupied. It was papered with the most virulent of greens, exhaling that peculiar odour resembling onions, which distinguishes arsenical papers when shut up; and the room having no fireplace, the unfortunate inmate had had no chance of battling with 'Death on the walls.' The verdict was unquestionable; but it came too late to save the life of an invaluable servant, who shortly after this expired."

"That is probably only one case out of a thousand," said Mr. Herbert, "where death has been caused, not by wilful negligence, but by ignorance. It is singular how much plainness of speech is needed in the matter. I went one evening to visit an acquaintance, and on being shown into the drawing-room, found, to my dismay, a pale green paper. Upon venturing to warn my hostess, she said, 'Do you think there can be any harm in this shade? I have the greatest horror of arsenic, having had erysipelas in consequence of wearing a green wreath. I have certainly not been well since we had this room repapered, but I had no idea this light shade could be arsenical.'"

"I could cap your story with many similar ones," said Sir Robert; "but look! just now Mont Blanc is beginning to assume his chameleon robe of varied tints, previous to reposing in the ashy pallor of night. And as we leave to-morrow for Geneva, let us drink in the solemn scene once more, with awe-struck silence, and bow before the Monarch of mountains.'

CHAPTER XVIII.

OUR PARTING.

"Magna est veritas, et prevalebit."

Geneva.

"Our pleasant party is broken up," said Mr. Fortescue, as he joined Lord Henry on the balcony of the Metropole, and found him scrutinizing the Jardin Anglais. "Chichester leaves us this evening."

"Indeed," said Lord Henry. "I was just going to propose crossing the lake to Nyon, that we might feast our eyes upon the sunset glories which irradiate Mont Blanc as seen from thence. A lady has been most enthusiastically expatiating upon them. What hurries Chichester away? But here he comes to speak for himself."

"I have received some letters which were awaiting me at the post office," answered Sir R. Chichester, "and I find I must return to England at once. I should much have liked to have explored the environs of Geneva, and to have visited Lausanne and Chillon with you both; to have heard once more the wondrous strains of the Freiburg organ, and to have crossed the Jura; but now I must take the shortest route homeward, *vid* Lyons, and bid you adieu this evening."

"Well, my dear fellow, we shall be sorry to lose you," said Lord Henry, "for you have helped to make our excursion very agreeable; but you will have the satisfaction of recalling a great triumph in connexion with it, and feeling that you have succeeded in arousing the interest and overcoming the indifference of both Fortescue and myself upon the subject you have so much at heart. When first you arraigned green paper as a prisoner at the bar, I believe we both rather expected to be self-retained as its advocates; but now, as far as we are concerned, I really fear judgment must go by default."

"You are very good to say so," returned his friend; "and I have no doubt but that, now your attention has been drawn to it, you will have many opportunities, if not of saving life, yet of arresting mischief by ventilating the subject."

"Percy Herbert told me one or two curious incidents which corroborate what you say," remarked Mr. Fortescue. " He was requested to visit a worthy old woman who had recently removed from the Strand into his parish. Herbert went and found all tidy, and herself evidently well cared for, but the green of the period on the walls. He said nothing, hoping she might not be susceptible to its influence, but made his visits as short as possible. In about three weeks the old lady remarked, 'It is very strange, sir, this neighbourhood is so much higher and better than what I have been living in before, and yet I have not felt half so well since we have moved up here. My niece is afraid we shall not be able to stop.'

"Herbert assured her the air was innocent enough, but added, 'I should be ill myself if I were to sleep in this room one night.' The old lady looked amazed; and, while he was unravelling the mystery to her, her niece entered, and, after hearing his story, asked if it could possibly account for the fact that she and her husband always awoke with sore throats, their room being similarly adorned. They had given notice to quit, but now lost no time in removing the noxious papers instead, and soon found no reason to quarrel with their new situation.

Ever after they used to say Herbert had saved the old lady's life."

"Lady Chichester often meets with such cases in her frequent visits amongst the poor in London," said her husband. "Those employed in paper-hanging are, however, almost invariably alive to the danger. Once she went to see a poor family, and found them, as she thought, in the bustle of a removal. On inquiry, she found that the landlady had repapered the room they occupied, with a bright green paper the day before. It was intended as a pleasant surprise to the man on his return from his day's work, and the wife had worked hard to have the room like a new pin before he came home. No sooner did he see the colour than he told her nothing should induce him to sleep in it one night; nor did he. His wife said he only wished he never had to put up those papers for other people."

"It would be trifling indeed with health to encounter the risk when aware of the danger," said Mr. Fortescue; "but I suppose for the most part people do so ignorantly."

"Yes, and that is why one should everywhere make known the danger. Only lately I received a letter from a lady in Dublin. She had gone there to nurse a little nephew ill in what they called rheumatic fever. While sitting beside his bed, and watching the strange phases and changes in his malady, she noticed that his bedroom paper was a light green, and, remembering my case, instantly wrote to inquire if this could have caused his illness. Whether it had done so or not, I urged her not to trifle with it, but to have him removed into another room. He was deemed too ill to try the experiment that day, but his removal was effected on the day following, and a change for the better was perceptible in a few hours. Now, had I not given her my own story, it would never have occurred to her that the poor child was being slowly poisoned, and in a few days more he might have been lost to his parents."

"It will be a singular sequel to our tour," said Lord Henry, musingly, "if, when one gets back, one is able to throw light upon some unaccountable illness amongst one's friends, or to unravel some case which has baffled medical skill. You have often been thus fortunate, Chichester?"

"Yes, because it is naturally my first question, when I find any otherwise inexplicable illness. The melancholy thing is when one comes too late; when, without stating one's own fears as to the cause of some painful bereavement in a friend's circle, you tell your story, and at length see conviction flash across him that his wife or favourite child might have been spared but for this fatal danger, hitherto unknown to him. This has occurred to myself more than once, and occasioned many a mental vow that no one within the pale of my acquaintance should be able to lay such misprision of treason at my door—that if the poisoner *must* stalk the land unchecked, my friends shall at least be warned."

"You feel strongly on the subject, Chichester," said Lord Henry.

"I have myself so narrowly escaped from the jaws of death, and seen so many from the same cause unconsciously nearing that bourne whence no traveller returns," replied Sir Robert, "that I should be a traitor were I to withhold my knowledge, or suffer the foe to steal in unawares. I will give you another instance of the necessity for being on the alert. Not long ago, when at Tunbridge Wells, I heard that an old acquaintance had taken a beautiful place in the immediate neighbourhood, and went to call. I found only a young lady at home, who told me that her father had removed thither on account of her health. She had long been delicate, and it was supposed that London, where they chiefly resided, did not suit her. But she added, 'I am sorry now that he has done so, for though when we were formerly staying here the air seemed like life to me, I have never been well since we settled here. I grieve that my father should have given up such a nice house and gone to such expense for nothing.'

"It was painful to see such a melancholy expression in one so young, and as my eye is now pretty well practised in detecting traces of arsenic, I thought I saw them in her countenance. 'Have you any green paper in the house?' I asked. She thought there was, in her mother's sitting-room, and invited me to inspect it. The green of the period was unmistakably there. 'Did I think *that* could cause her illness, it was so pretty a shade?' she said. By degrees she recollected that she had the same paper in her bedroom, and that in these two rooms she passed most of her time; also that, in their house in Hyde Park, green paper had likewise adorned the rooms she occupied, and where latterly she had never known a day's health."

"How passing strange that no medical man had discovered all this before you did," said Mr. Fortescue, "for of course she was under the doctor's hands?"

"She was so," said Sir Robert, "for she remarked that her doctor's own expression was, that her blood had been poisoned, but he could not find out the cause, and he had just urged her father to take her away for change of air."

"Was the paper removed?" asked Lord Henry.

"Immediately," replied Sir Robert, "and with it many of her distressing sensations disappeared. It requires, however, a long course of antidotes, or a long process of elimination, in such a case as hers, to eradicate the poison entirely."

"Do you always find your friends equally amenable to reason?" inquired Mr. Fortescue.

"Far from it. I remember warning a gentleman on the subject, who thought it sufficient to remark, with a smile, that it was in his children's playroom, and in other rooms of the house. Three months later I was shocked to learn that one of his children, a fine little fellow, had been carried off by diphtheria, after only a week's illness.

"On another occasion," continued Sir Robert Chichester, "when visiting an old friend, some difficulty arose in finding a bedroom for me, nearly all being hung with entirely green paper. Lady Maude, my amiable hostess, was altogether unaware of the dangerous properties of the green of the period, and I think would have taken my advice in banishing it from at least her own bedroom, but for the supreme contempt thrown upon my views by her nephew. The paper accordingly remained. Within a twelvemonth she was, without any assignable cause, attacked by paralysis, and has remained ever since hopelessly affected."

"So much for trifling with known poison," said Lord Henry. "Perhaps, Chichester, when next we meet, we shall be able to interchange strange adventures of ourselves or friends, in encountering this traitor in the camp. For who knows but that oftentimes its victims may have attributed its baneful effects to any and every cause but the right?"

"I have no hesitation in saying that such results must be of constant occurrence," replied Sir Robert; "and it is surely better to know one's foe than to run full tilt at the enemy in the dark. But it is against wilful ignorance that I plant my heavy artillery. Some months since, I paid a visit to a county hospital, and was shown all over the large and well-ordered establishment. Alas! even there the Englishman's darling—the poisoner—was lurking. In the matron's parlour, where a convalescent patient was sitting (kindly invited down for change of air), and in many of the adjacent rooms and offices opening into the same passage, I saw the green of the period, and drew attention to the mischief. I shall not soon forget the supercilious disdain with which my remarks were received by the matron. It was evidently not the first time similar ones had been laid before her. Still, there was reason on her side; for, as she intimated, at a hospital where all the principal medical men of the city attended, it was carrying coals to Newcastle with a vengeance, for a humble individual like myself to proffer any sanitary suggestions."

"What a pity those medicos do not take a lesson from the homœopathists in admitting the power of infinitesimals," said Lord Henry, "even if they class the mischief under that head."

"Indeed it is so," said Sir Robert. "Just before leaving England, I met a man whose eyes had been opened to the danger in question by a process almost as rough as that which enlightened my own, and who was in consequence equally susceptible to the influence of arsenic. He told me he had been on a visit to his brother, having first bargained for exemption from arsenical surroundings. He found his bedroom paper so nearly white that it needed a detective's skill to discover a tiny green seaweed pervading it. He tried to shut his eyes to an indication so slight, but, after struggling against it for a night or two, he was obliged to ask for another room, where he was assured that nothing of the sort existed. Alas! in the pattern there lurked a small spot, which, multiplied some two or three thousand times, contained perhaps some two or three hundred grains of arsenic. Unwilling to create a disturbance, he slept with a handkerchief over his face, and so passed the first night. His second essay was less successful, and, after combating with restlessness, sickness, heart-burning, and sore throat, and feeling altogether wretchedly ill, he had to succumb to the foe, and beat a retreat at 2 a.m. to the dining-room, where in about an hour all these symptoms vanished, and, having established his quarters on the sofa, he slept soundly till aroused by the astonished housemaids. It is needless to say he ran no further risks; and it is as needless to add that we both agreed that thousands of times similar sufferings were unjustly laid at the door of climate, or food, which were simply attributable to the green of the period."

"This thought should commend your researches at all events to the owners of property, as well as to lodging-house keepers," said Mr. Fortescue. "I have no doubt but that, being on the true scent, we shall now find your verdant assassin where one would least expect it. For instance, I have an idea that I have seen green paper frequently at railway stations."

"Very probably," returned Sir Robert. "I could name whole lines where in the waiting-rooms of each station you would find the arsenical green of the period. At many of these I have known the attendants, when questioned, complain of sore throats."

"The fact is," added Sir Robert, "it is in no sense an *ignis fatuus* against which I wage war. Facts are stubborn things. In private houses and in public halls; in palatial hotels and at wayside inns; in county hospitals and in private asylums; at railway stations and in doctors' waiting-rooms; in artists' studios and in hair-dressing saloons; in convalescent hospitals and in model lodging-houses; in nurseries and schoolrooms; in boardrooms and committee-rooms; in restaurants, offices, and shops; in mansions of the rich and in cottages of the poor, this deadly poison with its bewitching green dress is silently doing its work. Yet give me but a fulcrum for my lever, and I should not despair of arousing England to a conviction of its danger as completely as you are good enough to say I already have two of her noble scions."

"I bow to the fact and the compliment," said Lord Henry; "and now, how shall we aid you? Fortescue, suppose we get Chichester to write an account of our travels (omitting, however, particulars of our tour and *détours*, which must be visited to be appreciated, and all the lore, historical and legendary, which we have gleaned by the way), but confining himself to the important disquisitions which have so often come on the *tapis*."

"I have been repeatedly urged to write upon the subject," replied Sir Robert; "amongst others by the late Dr. Elliotson, but how, in combating prejudice, can I ensure readers?"

"Well, put me down for any reasonable number of copies, my dear fellow," said Lord Henry, "and I will do my best to extend our newly acquired knowledge."

"I endorse Henry Douglass' promise in each particular," said Mr. Fortescue. "It is, indeed, the least return we can make you for having opened our eyes, and averted possible danger from ourselves or our families."

"Thanks, my dear friends! I only hope all whose minds have become alive to the subject, whether by the logic of facts, or by practical experience, will follow your good example. Then I shall rest assured of success. Meanwhile, time now warns me to prepare for my departure; but, stimulated by your encouragement, I will make the attempt, and strive to rid England of

"THE GREEN OF THE PERIOD."

APPENDIX.

A (page 33).

"It is futile to bring forward instances of exemption against the unanswerable facts adduced of illness produced by inhabiting chambers papered with Scheele's green, and the disappearance of such illnesses on the removal of the papers."—*The British and Foreign Medico-Chirurgical Review*, No. LVII., p. 133.

B (page 34).

"Dr. Letheby's examination of the paper revealed the fact that *no less than one-third of its whole weight consisted of arsenite of copper!*

"Dr. Taylor found in another sample of green paper 59 per cent. of the arsenite. The same authority reports that the quantity consumed weekly by one manufacturer is two tons!"—*Ibid.*, p. 133.

C (page 124).

Contrary to the popular fallacy that the only danger to be apprehended from arsenical papers is confined to green *flock* paper, we learn from the *Quarterly Medical Journal* that, "The 'flock' of green paper is not coloured with arsenite of copper, nor with chromate of lead, or any other 'body colour,' but is simply wool dyed with *grains d'Avignon*, French berries, which are indigenous in France. . . . So that the *ground of a flock-paper is the only part which contains arsenic.*"—*Ibid.*, p. 133.

D (page 150).

OPHTHALMIA A RESULT OF THE USE OF ARSENICAL WALL-PAPERS.

BY DR. ALFRED S. TAYLOR.

As it is now a demonstrable fact that a fine dust, or powder containing arsenic, is evolved from the walls of rooms which are covered with arsenical or *emerald-green* papers, it becomes a question whether some obscure cases of inflammation of the conjunctiva may not be traced to this cause. Arsenic, it is well known, has a powerful action on the mucous membrane: when taken in small doses at intervals, one of its marked effects consists in producing irritation and inflammation of the conjunctiva, as well as of the membrane of the nose and fauces. These symptoms have been frequently observed in chronic poisoning by arsenic. The following case of a friend appears to support the view that exposure to an atmosphere containing an arsenical compound diffused through it, may produce this symptom of chronic poisoning by arsenic. I here quote the words of my friend as contained in his letter to me, dated January 9th, 1858. In reference to his library or sitting-room, he says:—

"The library was papered in 1853 with a brilliant green flock-paper, but, owing to the bad draught of the chimney, one of the windows was generally kept open, with or without a fire. This naturally prevented my using the room much; but about a year or more afterwards the defect seemed to cure itself, and it has not since given the same inconvenience. I on two occasions made a more than ordinary use of the room. The first time was during the winter of 1856-7, when my mother was abroad, and it was my only sitting-room; and the second time was during the spring of 1858, when I was busy with some literary work. Both these occasions were followed by an attack of illness, consisting of great depression, a want of interest in anything, a husky feeling in the throat, and a soreness and irritability in the eyes. It was not until you analyzed my paper in the summer of 1858 that I was aware of its containing arsenic. I then ordered it to be pulled down, which was done while I was in lodgings. I had, however, the book-cases carefully covered with thick cloths to prevent the oak being splashed by the decorators, and these cloths were not removed until the new papering was completed. The paper was, I believe, removed by wetting it, so that no dust would be created in the operation. We may safely, therefore, assume that any dust in the book-cases, which are all glazed, must have been there before the papering was altered. After my gradual recovery from my attack of illness in the summer, my eyes were comparatively quiet until my return to town, when I took possession of my new room, and commenced dusting the books in the book-cases, which had probably not been thoroughly dusted for two or three years. After dusting several of the cases I was again troubled with inflammation of the eyes, which made me think of the possible effect of the dust. I therefore discontinued operations, and gradually recovered. I left two book-cases undisturbed, from one of which you will remember that we obtained the dust which you lately analyzed."

It was the discovery of arsenic in comparatively large quantity in this dust which led me to institute further inquiries, resulting in the discovery that the green arsenical pigment must, when the paper is unglazed, be continually escaping in an impalpable powder from the wall. An optician, from whose shop I obtained additional evidence of the escape of the green pigment from the walls, informed me that the eyes of the men employed to hang the paper were affected, although at that time he had no suspicion of the cause.

When I saw my friend (whose case is above related), pending the second attack, the conjunctiva of the lids was of a deep red colour, along the tarsal margins and at the angles. The lids were slightly tumid, and had a tendency to eversion. Vision was painful. It was the apparent connexion of this second attack with the dusting of the books which led him to request me to examine the dust.

Since that time I have received several communications on the subject, bearing out the view that this insidious form of arsenical poisoning may be productive of inflammation of the conjunctiva. A medical practitioner resident in the country, since his occupation of one of these arsenical chambers for a few months, had suffered from mucous derangement of the bowels, colic, and inflammation of the tarsal portions of the conjunctiva. I examined the wall-paper, and found it loaded with arsenic, coarsely laid on and easily detached by the slightest friction. A well-known member of the profession in London, who has published his own case, informed me that he had been out of health since he had occupied a room of which the walls were covered with a green paper, and that he had suffered from inflammation of the eyes. I found arsenic in the dust collected from the picture-frames hung in the room.

These facts appear to show a close relation of cause and effect. It is said that the men who manufacture the paper do not suffer; but, so far as I can ascertain, the colour is ground and well mixed with water. It is laid on the wall-paper in a wet state, and thus the workmen are not exposed to the same amount of risk as those who live in chambers where the paper is hung in a dry state, and where, from the porous nature of the composition (whiting and arsenical green) changes in humidity and temperature may lead to the separation of portions of the noxious pigment. The glazing or sizing of the paper may to some extent prevent these accidents, by giving a more permanent fixing to the material.

A well-known manufacturer of "night-lights" in London informed me that when the green (arsenical) paper was used for wrapping the night-lights, the men who cut the papers suffered very much in their eyes, and could only work at it a few hours. I informed him that the use of this pigment for night-lights was very dangerous, since the smouldering of the paper in a close room might produce serious effects. He now uses other and innocent colours.

I believe that the first attack of inflammation of the eyes from which my friend suffered was the result of the *constitutiona* effects of slow poisoning. I give this opinion because there were other symptoms from which he suffered also indicative of the constitutional effects of arsenic. The second attack was probably dependent on the *local* action of the arsenical dust. It came on *rapidly*, and was not, so far as I am informed, attended with the other constitutional symptoms. In the two other cases, of medical men, referred to in my paper, the whole of the facts point to a *constitutional* action of the arsenical dust bringing on an attack of inflammation of the conjunctiva *gradually*.

This probable cause of one form of ophthalmia is worthy of the notice of ophthalmic surgeons.

Printed in the United States
128376LV00004B/134/A